Strategic Policy Interactions in a Monetary Union

Michael Carlberg

Strategic Policy Interactions
in a Monetary Union

Professor Dr. Michael Carlberg
Helmut Schmidt University
Federal University of Hamburg
Holstenhofweg 85
22043 Hamburg
Germany
michael.carlberg@hsuhh.de

ISBN 978-3-540-92750-1   e-ISBN 978-3-540-92751-8

DOI 10.1007/978-3-540-92751-8

Library of Congress Control Number: 2009922255

© Springer-Verlag Berlin Heidelberg 2009

This work is subject to copyright. All rights are reserved, whether the whole or part of the material is concerned, specifically the rights of translation, reprinting, reuse of illustrations, recitation, broadcasting, reproduction on microfilm or in any other way, and storage in data banks. Duplication of this publication or parts thereof is permitted only under the provisions of the German Copyright Law of September 9, 1965, in its current version, and permissions for use must always be obtained from Springer-Verlag. Violations are liable for prosecution under the German Copyright Law.

The use of general descriptive names, registered names, trademarks, etc. in this publication does not imply, even in the absence of a specific statement, that such names are exempt from the relevant protective laws and regulations and therefore free for general use.

Cover design: WMX Design GmbH Heidelberg

Printed on acid-free paper

springer.com

Preface

This book studies the strategic policy interactions in a monetary union. The leading protagonists are the European Central Bank and national governments. The target of the ECB is low inflation in Europe. The targets of a national government are low unemployment and a low structural deficit. There are demand shocks, supply shocks, and mixed shocks. There are country-specific shocks and common shocks. This book develops a series of basic, intermediate, and more advanced models. Here the focus is on the Nash equilibrium. The key questions are: Given a shock, can policy interactions reduce the existing loss? And to what extent can they do so? Another topical issue is policy cooperation. To illustrate all of this there are a lot of numerical examples.

The present book is part of a larger research project on European Monetary Union, see the references given at the back of the book. Some parts of this project were presented at the World Congress of the International Economic Association, at the International Conference on Macroeconomic Analysis, at the International Institute of Public Finance, and at the International Atlantic Economic Conference. Other parts were presented at the Macro Study Group of the German Economic Association, at the Annual Meeting of the Austrian Economic Association, at the Göttingen Workshop on International Economics, at the Halle Workshop on Monetary Economics, at the Research Seminar on Macroeconomics in Freiburg, at the Research Seminar on Economics in Kassel, and at the Passau Workshop on International Economics.

Over the years, in working on this project, I have benefited from comments by Iain Begg, Michael Bräuninger, Volker Clausen, Valeria de Bonis, Peter Flaschel, Helmut Frisch, Wilfried Fuhrmann, Franz X. Hof, Florence Huart, Oliver Landmann, Jay H. Levin, Alfred Maußner, Jochen Michaelis, Reinhard Neck, Manfred J. M. Neumann, Klaus Neusser, Franco Reither, Armin Rohde,

Sergio Rossi, Gerhard Rübel, Michael Schmid, Gerhard Schwödiauer, Dennis Snower, Egbert Sturm, Patrizio Tirelli, Harald Uhlig, Bas van Aarle, Uwe Vollmer, Jürgen von Hagen and Helmut Wagner. In addition, Christian Gäckle, Arne Hansen and Mirko Hoppe carefully discussed with me all parts of the manuscript. Last but not least, Christine Bergner did the secretarial work as excellently as ever. I would like to thank all of them.

Michael Carlberg

Executive Summary

1) Interaction between the European central bank, the German government, and the French government. First consider the framework of analysis. The targets of the European central bank are zero inflation in Germany and France. The instrument of the European central bank is European money supply. The European central bank has a quadratic loss function. The targets of the German government are zero unemployment and a zero structural deficit in Germany. The instrument of the German government is German government purchases. The German government has a quadratic loss function. The targets of the French government are zero unemployment and a zero structural deficit in France. The instrument of the French government is French government purchases. The French government has a quadratic loss function. The Nash equilibrium is determined by the reaction functions of the European central bank, the German government, and the French government. It yields the equilibrium levels of European money supply, German government purchases, and French government purchases.

Second consider a common demand shock in Europe. As a result, policy interaction can achieve zero inflation, zero unemployment, and a zero structural deficit in each of the member countries. Third consider a common supply shock in Europe. As a result, policy interaction can achieve zero inflation in each of the member countries. On the other hand, it causes an increase in both unemployment and the structural deficit.

Fourth consider a demand shock in Germany. As a result, policy interaction can achieve zero inflation, zero unemployment, and a zero structural deficit in Europe as a whole. However, it cannot do so in each of the member countries. Fifth consider a supply shock in Germany. As a result, policy interaction can achieve zero inflation in Europe as a whole. On the other hand, it causes an increase in both unemployment and the structural deficit.

2) Cooperation between the European central bank, the German government, and the French government. First consider the framework of analysis. The targets

of policy cooperation are zero inflation, zero unemployment, and a zero structural deficit in each of the member countries. The instruments of policy cooperation are European money supply, German government purchases, and French government purchases. The policy makers agree on a common loss function. The cooperative equilibrium is determined by the first-order conditions for a minimum loss. It yields the optimum levels of European money supply, German government purchases, and French government purchases.

Second consider a common demand shock in Europe. As a result, policy cooperation can achieve zero inflation, zero unemployment, and a zero structural deficit in each of the member countries. Third consider a common supply shock in Europe. As a result, policy cooperation is ineffective.

Fourth consider a demand shock in Germany. As a result, policy cooperation can achieve zero inflation, zero unemployment, and a zero structural deficit in Europe as a whole. However, it cannot do so in each of the member countries. Fifth consider a supply shock in Germany. As a result, policy cooperation is ineffective. Sixth consider a mixed shock in Germany. As a result, policy cooperation can reduce the loss to a certain extent.

Contents in Brief

Introduction 1

Part One. The Monetary Union as a Whole: Absence of a Deficit Target 13
Chapter 1. Monetary Policy A 15
Chapter 2. Monetary Policy B 20
Chapter 3. Fiscal Policy A 27
Chapter 4. Fiscal Policy B 32
Chapter 5. Interaction between Central Bank and Government 37
Chapter 6. Cooperation between Central Bank and Government 43
Chapter 7. Interaction between Central Bank and Government:
　　　　　A Special Case 50

Part Two. The Monetary Union as a Whole: Presence of a Deficit Target 57
Chapter 1. Fiscal Policy A 59
Chapter 2. Fiscal Policy B 65
Chapter 3. Interaction between Central Bank and Government A 70
Chapter 4. Interaction between Central Bank and Government B 77
Chapter 5. Interaction between Central Bank and Government C 83
Chapter 6. Cooperation between Central Bank and Government 90

Part Three. The Monetary Union of Two Countries: Absence of a Deficit Target 95
Chapter 1. Monetary Policy in Europe A 97
Chapter 2. Monetary Policy in Europe B 106
Chapter 3. Fiscal Policy in Germany A 114
Chapter 4. Fiscal Policy in Germany B 119

Chapter 5. Interaction between European Central Bank,
  German Government, and French Government 124
Chapter 6. Cooperation between European Central Bank,
  German Government, and French Government 132

Part Four. The Monetary Union of Two Countries: Presence of a Deficit Target 141

Chapter 1. Fiscal Policy in Germany A 143
Chapter 2. Fiscal Policy in Germany B 149
Chapter 3. Interaction between European Central Bank,
  German Government, and French Government A 154
Chapter 4. Interaction between European Central Bank,
  German Government, and French Government B 169
Chapter 5. Interaction between European Central Bank,
  German Government, and French Government C 181
Chapter 6. Cooperation between European Central Bank,
  German Government, and French Government 193

Synopsis 204
Conclusion 207
Result 229
Symbols 235
The Current Research Project 237
References 241
Index 253

Contents

Introduction 1
1. Subject and Approach 1
2. The Monetary Union as a Whole:
   Absence of a Deficit Target 3
3. The Monetary Union as a Whole:
   Presence of a Deficit Target 5
4. The Monetary Union of Two Countries:
   Absence of a Deficit Target 7
5. The Monetary Union of Two Countries:
   Presence of a Deficit Target 10

**Part One. The Monetary Union as a Whole:
Absence of a Deficit Target** 13

Chapter 1. Monetary Policy A 15
1. The Model 15
2. Some Numerical Examples 17
   2.1. A Demand Shock in Europe 17
   2.2. A Supply Shock in Europe 18

Chapter 2. Monetary Policy B 20
1. The Model 20
2. Some Numerical Examples 22
   2.1. A Demand Shock in Europe 22
   2.2. A Supply Shock in Europe 23
   2.3. A Mixed Shock in Europe 24
   2.4. Another Mixed Shock in Europe 24

Chapter 3. Fiscal Policy A 27
1. The Model 27
2. Some Numerical Examples 29
   2.1. A Demand Shock in Europe 29
   2.2. A Supply Shock in Europe 30

Chapter 4. Fiscal Policy B 32
1. The Model 32
2. Some Numerical Examples 34

Chapter 5. Interaction between Central Bank and Government 37

Chapter 6. Cooperation between Central Bank and Government 43
1. The Model 43
2. Some Numerical Examples 46
   2.1. A Demand Shock in Europe 46
   2.2. A Supply Shock in Europe 47
   2.3. A Mixed Shock in Europe 48

Chapter 7. Interaction between Central Bank and Government:
  A Special Case 50
1. The Model 50
2. Some Numerical Examples 52

Part Two. The Monetary Union as a Whole: Presence of a Deficit Target 57

Chapter 1. Fiscal Policy A 59
1. The Model 59
2. Some Numerical Examples 62
   2.1. A Demand Shock in Europe 62
   2.2. A Supply Shock in Europe 63

Chapter 2. Fiscal Policy B 65
1. The Model 65
2. Some Numerical Examples 66

Chapter 3. Interaction between Central Bank and Government A 70
1. The Model 70
2. Some Numerical Examples 73
   2.1. A Demand Shock in Europe 74
   2.2. A Supply Shock in Europe 74

Chapter 4. Interaction between Central Bank and Government B 77
1. The Model 77
2. Some Numerical Examples 80

Chapter 5. Interaction between Central Bank and Government C 83
1. The Model 83
2. Some Numerical Examples 86

Chapter 6. Cooperation between Central Bank and Government 90
1. The Model 90
2. Some Numerical Examples 92
   2.1. A Demand Shock in Europe 92
   2.2. A Supply Shock in Europe 93

Part Three. The Monetary Union of Two Countries: Absence of a Deficit Target 95

Chapter 1. Monetary Policy in Europe A 97
1. The Model 97
2. Some Numerical Examples 101
   - 2.1. A Demand Shock in Germany 101
   - 2.2. A Supply Shock in Germany 102
   - 2.3. A Common Demand Shock in Europe 104

Chapter 2. Monetary Policy in Europe B 106
1. The Model 106
2. Some Numerical Examples 109

Chapter 3. Fiscal Policy in Germany A 114
1. The Model 114
2. Some Numerical Examples 116
   - 2.1. A Demand Shock in Germany 116
   - 2.2. A Supply Shock in Germany 117

Chapter 4. Fiscal Policy in Germany B 119
1. The Model 119
2. Some Numerical Examples 120

Chapter 5. Interaction between European Central Bank, German Government, and French Government 124

Chapter 6. Cooperation between European Central Bank, German Government, and French Government 132
1. The Model 132
2. Some Numerical Examples 136
   - 2.1. A Demand Shock in Germany 136
   - 2.2. A Supply Shock in Germany 138
   - 2.3. A Mixed Shock in Germany 138

Part Four. The Monetary Union of Two Countries: Presence of a Deficit Target 141

Chapter 1. Fiscal Policy in Germany A 143
1. The Model 143
2. Some Numerical Examples 145
   2.1. A Demand Shock in Germany 146
   2.2. A Supply Shock in Germany 147

Chapter 2. Fiscal Policy in Germany B 149
1. The Model 149
2. Some Numerical Examples 150

Chapter 3. Interaction between European Central Bank, German Government, and French Government A 154
1. The Model 154
2. Some Numerical Examples 161
   2.1. A Demand Shock in Germany 161
   2.2. A Supply Shock in Germany 163
   2.3. A Common Demand Shock in Europe 165
   2.4. A Common Supply Shock in Europe 166

Chapter 4. Interaction between European Central Bank, German Government, and French Government B 169
1. The Model 169
2. Some Numerical Examples 174

Chapter 5. Interaction between European Central Bank, German Government, and French Government C 181
1. The Model 181
2. Some Numerical Examples 186

Chapter 6. Cooperation between European Central Bank, German Government, and French Government 193
1. The Model 193
2. Some Numerical Examples 197

Synopsis 204

Conclusion 207
1. The Monetary Union as a Whole:
   Absence of a Deficit Target 207
2. The Monetary Union as a Whole:
   Presence of a Deficit Target 211
3. The Monetary Union of Two Countries:
   Absence of a Deficit Target 216
4. The Monetary Union of Two Countries:
   Presence of a Deficit Target 221

Result 229
1. The Monetary Union of Two Countries:
   Absence of a Deficit Target 229
2. The Monetary Union of Two Countries:
   Presence of a Deficit Target 231

Symbols 235

The Current Research Project 237

References 241

Index 253

Introduction

1. Subject and Approach

This book studies the strategic policy interactions in a monetary union. Here the focus is on the Nash equilibrium. The monetary union consists of two countries, say Germany and France. The policy makers are the European central bank, the German government, and the French government.

An increase in European money supply lowers unemployment in Germany and France. On the other hand, it raises inflation there. However, it has no effect on structural deficits. An increase in German government purchases lowers unemployment in Germany. On the other hand, it raises inflation there. And what is more, is raises the structural deficit. Correspondingly, an increase in French government purchases lowers unemployment in France. On the other hand, it raises inflation there. And what is more, is raises the structural deficit.

The targets of the European central bank are zero inflation in Germany and France. The instrument of the European central bank is European money supply. There are two targets but only one instrument, so what is needed is a loss function. We assume that the European central bank has a quadratic loss function. The amount of loss depends on inflation in Germany and France. The European central bank sets European money supply so as to minimize its loss. The first-order condition for a minimum loss gives the reaction function of the European central bank. Suppose the German government raises German government purchases. Then, as a response, the European central bank lowers European money supply.

The targets of the German government are zero unemployment and a zero structural deficit in Germany. The instrument of the German government is German government purchases. There are two targets but only one instrument, so what is needed is a loss function. We assume that the German government has a quadratic loss function. The amount of loss depends on unemployment and the structural deficit in Germany. The German government sets German government purchases so as to minimize its loss. The first-order condition for a minimum loss gives the reaction function of the German government. Suppose the European central bank lowers European money supply. Then, as a response, the German government raises German government purchases.

Similarly, the targets of the French government are zero unemployment and a zero structural deficit in France. The instrument of the French government is French government purchases. There are two targets but only one instrument, so what is needed is a loss function. We assume that the French government has a quadratic loss function. The amount of loss depends on unemployment and the structural deficit in France. The French government sets French government purchases so as to minimize its loss. The first-order condition for a minimum loss gives the reaction function of the French government. Suppose the European central bank lowers European money supply. Then, as a response, the French government raises French government purchases.

The Nash equilibrium is determined by the reaction functions of the European central bank, the German government, and the French government. It yields the equilibrium levels of European money supply, German government purchases, and French government purchases. The key questions are: Given a shock, can monetary and fiscal interaction reduce the existing loss? And to what extent can it do so? To illustrate all of this there are numerical simulations of the Nash equilibrium.

This book consists of four major parts:
- The Monetary Union as a Whole: Absence of a Deficit Target
- The Monetary Union as a Whole: Presence of a Deficit Target
- The Monetary Union of Two Countries: Absence of a Deficit Target
- The Monetary Union of Two Countries: Presence of a Deficit Target.

Now the approach will be presented in greater detail.

2. The Monetary Union as a Whole: Absence of a Deficit Target

2.1. Interaction between Central Bank and Government

An increase in European money supply lowers unemployment in Europe. On the other hand, it raises inflation there. Correspondingly, an increase in European government purchases lowers unemployment in Europe. On the other hand, it raises inflation there.

In the numerical example, a unit increase in money supply lowers the rate of unemployment by 1 percentage point. On the other hand, it raises the rate of inflation by 1 percentage point. Similarly, a unit increase in government purchases lowers the rate of unemployment by 1 percentage point. On the other hand, it raises the rate of inflation by 1 percentage point. For instance, let initial unemployment be 2 percent, and let initial inflation be 2 percent as well. Now consider a unit increase in money supply. Then unemployment goes from 2 to 1 percent. On the other hand, inflation goes from 2 to 3 percent.

The target of the European central bank is zero inflation in Europe. The instrument of the European central bank is European money supply. Thus there is one target and one instrument. We assume that the European central bank has a quadratic loss function. The amount of loss depends on the level of inflation. The European central bank sets European money supply so as to minimize its loss. The first-order condition for a minimum loss gives the reaction function of the European central bank. Suppose the European government raises European government purchases. Then, as a response, the European central bank lowers European money supply.

The target of the European government is zero unemployment in Europe. The instrument of the European government is European government purchases. Hence there is one target and one instrument. We assume that the European government has a quadratic loss function. The amount of loss depends on the level of unemployment. The European government sets European government purchases so as to minimize its loss. The first-order condition for a minimum loss gives the reaction function of the European government. Suppose the European central bank lowers European money supply. Then, as a response, the European government raises European government purchases.

The Nash equilibrium is determined by the reaction functions of the European central bank and the European government. It yields the equilibrium levels of European money supply and European government purchases. The key questions are: Does a Nash equilibrium exist? Are there multiple Nash equilibria? Is the Nash equilibrium Pareto efficient? Given a shock, can monetary and fiscal interaction reduce the existing loss? And to what extent can it do so? Of course, the answer depends on the type of shock. There are demand shocks, supply shocks, and mixed shocks.

2.2. Cooperation between Central Bank and Government

The policy makers are the European central bank and the European government. The targets of policy cooperation are zero inflation and zero unemployment in Europe. The instruments of policy cooperation are European money supply and European government purchases. Thus there are two targets and two instruments. We assume that the policy makers agree on a common loss function. The amount of loss depends on inflation and unemployment. The policy makers set European money supply and European government purchases so as to minimize the common loss.

The cooperative equilibrium is determined by the first-order conditions for a minimum loss. It yields the optimum combinations of European money supply and European government purchases. The key questions are: Does a cooperative equilibrium exist? Are there multiple equilibria? Given a shock, can monetary and fiscal cooperation reduce the existing loss? To what extent can it do so? Is policy cooperation superior to policy interaction?

3. The Monetary Union as a Whole: Presence of a Deficit Target

3.1. Interaction between Central Bank and Government

An increase in European money supply lowers unemployment in Europe. On the other hand, it raises inflation there. However, it has no effect on the structural deficit. Correspondingly, an increase in European government purchases lowers unemployment in Europe. On the other hand, it raises inflation there. And what is more, it raises the structural deficit.

In the numerical example, a unit increase in money supply lowers the rate of unemployment by 1 percentage point. On the other hand, it raises the rate of inflation by 1 percentage point. However, it has no effect on the structural deficit ratio. Similarly, a unit increase in government purchases lowers the rate of unemployment by 1 percentage point. On the other hand, it raises the rate of inflation by 1 percentage point. And what is more, it raises the structural deficit ratio by 1 percentage point. For instance, let initial unemployment be 2 percent, let initial inflation be 2 percent, and let the initial structural deficit be 2 percent as well. Now consider a unit increase in government purchases. Then unemployment goes from 2 to 1 percent. On the other hand, inflation goes from 2 to 3 percent. And what is more, the structural deficit goes from 2 to 3 percent as well.

The target of the European central bank is zero inflation in Europe. The instrument of the European central bank is European money supply. Thus there is one target and one instrument. We assume that the European central bank has a quadratic loss function. The amount of loss depends on the level of inflation. The European central bank sets European money supply so as to minimize its loss. Then the first-order condition for a minimum loss gives the reaction function of the European central bank.

The targets of the European government are zero unemployment and a zero structural deficit in Europe. The instrument of the European government is

European government purchases. There are two targets but only one instrument, so what is needed is a loss function. We assume that the European government has a quadratic loss function. The amount of loss depends on unemployment and the structural deficit in Europe. The European government sets European government purchases so as to minimize its loss. Then the first-order condition for a minimum loss gives the reaction function of the European government.

The Nash equilibrium is determined by the reaction functions of the European central bank and the European government. It yields the equilibrium levels of European money supply and European government purchases. The key questions are: Given a shock, can monetary and fiscal interaction reduce the existing loss? And to what extent can it do so?

3.2. Cooperation between Central Bank and Government

The policy makers are the European central bank and the European government. The targets of policy cooperation are zero inflation, zero unemployment, and a zero structural deficit. The instruments of policy cooperation are European money supply and European government purchases. There are three targets but only two instruments, so what is needed is a loss function. We assume that the policy makers agree on a common loss function. The amount of loss depends on inflation, unemployment, and the structural deficit. The policy makers set European money supply and European government purchases so as to minimize the common loss.

The cooperative equilibrium is determined by the first-order conditions for a minimum loss. It yields the optimum levels of European money supply and European government purchases. The key questions are: Given a shock, can monetary and fiscal cooperation reduce the existing loss? And to what extent can it do so?

4. The Monetary Union of Two Countries: Absence of a Deficit Target

4.1. Interaction between European Central Bank, German Government, and French Government

The monetary union consists of two countries, say Germany and France. The member countries are the same size and have the same behavioural functions. An increase in European money supply lowers unemployment in Germany and France. On the other hand, it raises inflation there. An increase in German government purchases lowers unemployment in Germany. On the other hand, it raises inflation there. Correspondingly, an increase in French government purchases lowers unemployment in France. On the other hand, it raises inflation there.

In the numerical example, a unit increase in European money supply lowers the rates of unemployment in Germany and France by 1 percentage point each. On the other hand, it raises the rates of inflation there by 1 percentage point each. A unit increase in German government purchases lowers the rate of unemployment in Germany by 1 percentage point. On the other hand, it raises the rate of inflation there by 1 percentage point. Similarly, a unit increase in French government purchases lowers the rate of unemployment in France by 1 percentage point. On the other hand, it raises the rate of inflation there by 1 percentage point.

For instance, let initial unemployment in Germany be 3 percent, and let initial unemployment in France be 1 percent. Further let initial inflation in Germany be 3 percent, and let initial inflation in France be 1 percent. Now consider a unit increase in European money supply. Then unemployment in Germany goes from 3 to 2 percent, and unemployment in France goes from 1 to zero percent. On the other hand, inflation in Germany goes from 3 to 4 percent, and inflation in France goes from 1 to 2 percent.

The targets of the European central bank are zero inflation in Germany and France. The instrument of the European central bank is European money supply. There are two targets but only one instrument, so what is needed is a loss function. We assume that the European central bank has a quadratic loss function. The amount of loss depends on inflation in Germany and France. The European central bank sets European money supply so as to minimize its loss. The first-order condition for a minimum loss gives the reaction function of the European central bank. Suppose the German government raises German government purchases. Then, as a response, the European central bank lowers European money supply.

The target of the German government is zero unemployment in Germany. The instrument of the German government is German government purchases. Thus there is one target and one instrument. We assume that the German government has a quadratic loss function. The amount of loss depends on unemployment in Germany. The German government sets German government purchases so as to minimize its loss. The first-order condition for a minimum loss gives the reaction function of the German government. Suppose the European central bank lowers European money supply. Then, as a response, the German government raises German government purchases.

Correspondingly, the target of the French government is zero unemployment in France. The instrument of the French government is French government purchases. Hence there is one target and one instrument. We assume that the French government has a quadratic loss function. The amount of loss depends on unemployment in France. The French government sets French government purchases so as to minimize its loss. The first-order condition for a minimum loss gives the reaction function of the French government. Suppose the European central bank lowers European money supply. Then, as a response, the French government raises French government purchases.

The Nash equilibrium is determined by the reaction functions of the European central bank, the German government, and the French government. It yields the equilibrium levels of European money supply, German government purchases, and French government purchases. The key questions are: Does a Nash equilibrium exist? Are there multiple Nash equilibria? Is the Nash equilibrium Pareto efficient? Given a shock, can monetary and fiscal interaction reduce the existing loss? And to what extent can it do so? Of course, the answer depends on the type of shock. There are country-specific demand shocks, country-specific supply shocks, common demand shocks, and common supply shocks.

4.2. Cooperation between European Central Bank, German Government, and French Government

The policy makers are the European central bank, the German government, and the French government. The targets of policy cooperation are zero inflation and zero unemployment in each of the member countries. The instruments of policy cooperation are European money supply, German government purchases, and French government purchases. There are four targets but only three instruments, so what is needed is a loss function. We assume that the policy makers agree on a common loss function. The amount of loss depends on inflation and unemployment in each of the member countries. The policy makers set European money supply, German government purchases, and French government purchases so as to minimize the common loss.

The cooperative equilibrium is determined by the first-order conditions for a minimum loss. It yields the optimum combinations of European money supply, German government purchases, and French government purchases. The key questions are: Does a cooperative equilibrium exist? Are there multiple equilibria? Given a shock, can monetary and fiscal cooperation reduce the existing loss? And to what extent can it do so?

5. The Monetary Union of Two Countries: Presence of a Deficit Target

5.1. Interaction between European Central Bank, German Government, and French Government

An increase in European money supply lowers unemployment in Germany and France. On the other hand, it raises inflation there. However, it has no effect on structural deficits. An increase in German government purchases lowers unemployment in Germany. On the other hand, it raises inflation there. And what is more, it raises the structural deficit. Correspondingly, an increase in French government purchases lowers unemployment in France. On the other hand, it raises inflation there. And what is more, it raises the structural deficit.

In the numerical example, a unit increase in European money supply lowers the rates of unemployment in Germany and France by 1 percentage point each. On the other hand, it raises the rates of inflation there by 1 percentage point each. However, it has no effect on the structural deficit ratios there. A unit increase in German government purchases lowers the rate of unemployment in Germany by 1 percentage point. On the other hand, it raises the rate of inflation there by 1 percentage point. And what is more, it raises the structural deficit ratio there by 1 percentage point as well. Similarly, a unit increase in French government purchases lowers the rate of unemployment in France by 1 percentage point. On the other hand, it raises the rate of inflation there by 1 percentage point. And what is more, it raises the structural deficit ratio there by 1 percentage point as well.

For instance, let initial unemployment in Germany be 2 percent, let initial inflation in Germany be 2 percent, and let the initial structural deficit in Germany be 2 percent as well. Now consider a unit increase in German government purchases. Then unemployment in Germany goes from 2 to 1 percent. On the other hand, inflation in Germany goes from 2 to 3 percent. And what is more, the structural deficit in Germany goes from 2 to 3 percent as well.

The targets of the European central bank are zero inflation in Germany and France. The instrument of the European central bank is European money supply. There are two targets but only one instrument, so what is needed is a loss function. We assume that the European central bank has a quadratic loss function. The amount of loss depends on inflation in Germany and France. The European central bank sets European money supply so as to minimize its loss. Then the first-order condition for a minimum loss gives the reaction function of the European central bank.

The targets of the German government are zero unemployment and a zero structural deficit in Germany. The instrument of the German government is German government purchases. There are two targets but only one instrument, so what is needed is a loss function. We assume that the European central bank has a quadratic loss function. The amount of loss depends on unemployment and the structural deficit in Germany. The German government sets German government purchases so as to minimize its loss. Then the first-order condition for a minimum loss gives the reaction function of the German government.

The targets of the French government are zero unemployment and a zero structural deficit in France. The instrument of the French government is French government purchases. There are two targets but only one instrument, so what is needed is a loss function. We assume that the French government has a quadratic loss function. The amount of loss depends on unemployment and the structural deficit in France. The French government sets French government purchases so as to minimize its loss. Then the first-order condition for a minimum loss gives the reaction function of the French government.

The Nash equilibrium is determined by the reaction functions of the European central bank, the German government, and the French government. It yields the equilibrium levels of European money supply, German government purchases, and French government purchases. The key questions are: Given a shock, can monetary and fiscal interaction reduce the existing loss? And to what extent can it do so?

5.2. Cooperation between European Central Bank, German Government, and French Government

The policy makers are the European central bank, the German government, and the French government. The targets of policy cooperation are zero inflation, zero unemployment, and a zero structural deficit in each of the member countries. The instruments of policy cooperation are European money supply, German government purchases, and French government purchases. There are six targets but only three instruments, so what is needed is a loss function. We assume that the policy makers agree on a common loss function. The amount of loss depends on inflation, unemployment, and the structural deficit in each of the member countries. The policy makers set European money supply, German government purchases, and French government purchases so as to minimize the common loss.

The cooperative equilibrium is determined by the first-order conditions for a minimum loss. It yields the optimum levels of European money supply, German government purchases, and French government purchases. The key questions are: Given a shock, can monetary and fiscal cooperation reduce the existing loss? And to what extent can it do so?

Part One

The Monetary Union as a Whole

Absence of a Deficit Target

Chapter 1
Monetary Policy A

1. The Model

An increase in European money supply lowers unemployment in Europe. On the other hand, it raises inflation there. In the numerical example, a unit increase in money supply lowers the rate of unemployment by 1 percentage point. On the other hand, it raises the rate of inflation by 1 percentage point. For instance, let initial unemployment be 2 percent, and let initial inflation be 2 percent as well. Now consider a unit increase in money supply. Then unemployment goes from 2 to 1 percent. On the other hand, inflation goes from 2 to 3 percent.

The model of unemployment and inflation can be represented by a system of two equations:

$$u = A - \alpha M \tag{1}$$

$$\pi = B + \alpha \varepsilon M \tag{2}$$

Of course this is a reduced form. Here u denotes the rate of unemployment in Europe, π is the rate of inflation in Europe, M is European money supply, α is the monetary policy multiplier with respect to unemployment, $\alpha \varepsilon$ is the monetary policy multiplier with respect to inflation, A is some other factors bearing on the rate of unemployment in Europe, and B is some other factors bearing on the rate of inflation in Europe. The endogenous variables are the rate of unemployment and the rate of inflation in Europe.

According to equation (1), the rate of unemployment in Europe is a positive function of A and a negative function of European money supply. According to equation (2), the rate of inflation in Europe is a positive function of B and a positive function of European money supply. A unit increase in A raises the rate of unemployment by 1 percentage point. A unit increase in B raises the rate of inflation by 1 percentage point. A unit increase in money supply lowers the rate of unemployment by α percentage points. On the other hand, it raises the rate of inflation by αε percentage points.

As to policy targets there are two distinct cases. In case A the target of the central bank is zero inflation. In case B the targets of the central bank are zero inflation and zero unemployment. This chapter deals with case A, and the next chapter deals with case B.

The target of the European central bank is zero inflation in Europe. The instrument of the European central bank is European money supply. By equation (2), the optimum level of European money supply is:

$$M = -\frac{B}{\alpha\varepsilon} \tag{3}$$

That is, an increase in A requires no change in European money supply. And an increase in B requires a cut in European money supply. From equations (1) and (3) follows the optimum rate of unemployment in Europe:

$$u = \frac{\varepsilon A + B}{\varepsilon} \tag{4}$$

And from equations (2) and (3) follows the optimum rate of inflation in Europe:

$$\pi = 0 \tag{5}$$

Inflation in Europe is zero. By contrast, unemployment there is not zero.

2. Some Numerical Examples

For ease of exposition we assume that monetary policy multipliers are unity $\alpha = \varepsilon = 1$. On this assumption, the model of unemployment and inflation can be written as follows:

$$u = A - M \tag{1}$$
$$\pi = B + M \tag{2}$$

A unit increase in A raises the rate of unemployment by 1 percentage point. A unit increase in B raises the rate of inflation by 1 percentage point. A unit increase in money supply lowers the rate of unemployment by 1 percentage point. On the other hand, it raises the rate of inflation by 1 percentage point. The model can be solved this way:

$$M = -B \tag{3}$$
$$u = A + B \tag{4}$$
$$\pi = 0 \tag{5}$$

Equation (3) shows the optimum level of money supply, equation (4) shows the optimum rate of unemployment, and equation (5) shows the optimum rate of inflation.

It proves useful to study two distinct cases:
- a demand shock in Europe
- a supply shock in Europe.

1) A demand shock in Europe. Let initial unemployment be zero, and let initial inflation be zero as well. Step one refers to a decline in aggregate demand. In terms of the model there is an increase in A of 2 units and a decline in B of equally 2 units. Step two refers to the outside lag. Unemployment goes from zero to 2 percent. And inflation goes from zero to –2 percent. Step three refers to the policy response. What is needed, according to the model, is an increase in money

supply of 2 units. Step four refers to the outside lag. Inflation goes from −2 to zero percent. And unemployment goes from 2 to zero percent. Table 1.1 presents a synopsis.

As a result, given a demand shock, monetary policy can achieve zero inflation. And what is more, as a side effect, it can achieve zero unemployment. The loss function of the central bank is:

$$L_1 = \pi^2 \qquad (6)$$

The initial loss is zero. The demand shock causes a loss of 4 units. Then monetary policy can reduce the loss to zero.

2) A supply shock in Europe. Let initial unemployment and inflation be zero each. Step one refers to the supply shock. In terms of the model there is an increase in B of 2 units and an increase in A of equally 2 units. Step two refers to the outside lag. Inflation goes from zero to 2 percent. And unemployment goes from zero to 2 percent as well. Step three refers to the policy response. What is needed, according to the model, is a reduction in money supply of 2 units. Step four refers to the outside lag. Inflation goes from 2 to zero percent. And unemployment goes from 2 to 4 percent. Table 1.2 gives an overview.

As a result, given a supply shock, monetary policy can achieve zero inflation. However, as a side effect, it causes an increase in unemployment. The supply shock causes a loss of 4 units. Then monetary policy can reduce the loss to zero.

3) Summary. Given a demand shock, monetary policy can achieve zero inflation. And what is more, as a side effect, it can achieve zero unemployment. Given a supply shock, monetary policy can achieve zero inflation. However, as a side effect, it causes an increase in unemployment.

Table 1.1
Monetary Policy in Europe
A Demand Shock

Unemployment	0	Inflation	0
Shock in A	2	Shock in B	−2
Unemployment	2	Inflation	−2
Change in Money Supply	2		
Unemployment	0	Inflation	0

Table 1.2
Monetary Policy in Europe
A Supply Shock

Unemployment	0	Inflation	0
Shock in A	2	Shock in B	2
Unemployment	2	Inflation	2
Change in Money Supply	−2		
Unemployment	4	Inflation	0

Chapter 2
Monetary Policy B

1. The Model

The model of unemployment and inflation can be characterized by a system of two equations:

$$u = A - \alpha M \tag{1}$$

$$\pi = B + \alpha\varepsilon M \tag{2}$$

The targets of the European central bank are zero inflation and zero unemployment in Europe. The instrument of the European central bank is European money supply. There are two targets but only one instrument, so what is needed is a loss function. We assume that the European central bank has a quadratic loss function:

$$L_1 = \pi^2 + u^2 \tag{3}$$

L_1 is the loss to the European central bank caused by inflation and unemployment. For ease of exposition we assume equal weights in the loss function. The specific target of the European central bank is to minimize the loss, given the inflation function and the unemployment function. Taking account of equations (1) and (2), the loss function of the European central bank can be written as follows:

$$L_1 = (B + \alpha\varepsilon M)^2 + (A - \alpha M)^2 \tag{4}$$

Then the first-order condition for a minimum loss is:

$$M = \frac{A - \varepsilon B}{\alpha + \alpha\varepsilon^2} \tag{5}$$

Here M is the optimum level of European money supply. An increase in A requires an increase in European money supply. And an increase in B requires a cut in European money supply. From equations (1) and (5) follows the optimum rate of unemployment in Europe:

$$u = \frac{\varepsilon^2 A + \varepsilon B}{1 + \varepsilon^2} \qquad (6)$$

And from equations (2) and (5) follows the optimum rate of inflation in Europe:

$$\pi = \frac{\varepsilon A + B}{1 + \varepsilon^2} \qquad (7)$$

The comparison of equations (6) and (7) gives:

$$u = \varepsilon \pi \qquad (8)$$

Unemployment in Europe is not zero, nor is inflation there.

2. Some Numerical Examples

For ease of exposition we assume that monetary policy multipliers are unity $\alpha = \varepsilon = 1$. On this assumption, the model of unemployment and inflation can be written as follows:

$$u = A - M \qquad (1)$$
$$\pi = B + M \qquad (2)$$

A unit increase in money supply lowers the rate of unemployment by 1 percentage point. On the other hand, it raises the rate of inflation by 1 percentage point. The model can be solved this way:

$$2M = A - B \qquad (3)$$
$$2u = A + B \qquad (4)$$
$$2\pi = A + B \qquad (5)$$

Equation (3) shows the optimum level of money supply, equation (4) shows the optimum rate of unemployment, and equation (5) shows the optimum rate of inflation.

It proves useful to study four distinct cases:
- a demand shock in Europe
- a supply shock in Europe
- a mixed shock in Europe
- another mixed shock in Europe.

1) A demand shock in Europe. Let initial unemployment be zero, and let initial inflation be zero as well. Step one refers to a decline in aggregate demand. In terms of the model there is an increase in A of 2 units and a decline in B of equally 2 units. Step two refers to the outside lag. Unemployment goes from zero to 2 percent. And inflation goes from zero to –2 percent. Step three refers to the policy response. What is needed, according to the model, is an increase in money

supply of 2 units. Step four refers to the outside lag. Unemployment goes from 2 to zero percent. And inflation goes from –2 to zero percent. Table 1.3 presents a synopsis.

As a result, given a demand shock, monetary policy can achieve both zero inflation and zero unemployment. The loss function of the central bank is:

$$L_1 = \pi^2 + u^2 \tag{6}$$

The initial loss is zero. The demand shock causes a loss of 8 units. Then monetary policy can reduce the loss to zero.

Table 1.3
Monetary Policy in Europe
A Demand Shock

Unemployment	0	Inflation	0
Shock in A	2	Shock in B	– 2
Unemployment	2	Inflation	– 2
Change in Money Supply	2		
Unemployment	0	Inflation	0

2) A supply shock in Europe. Let initial unemployment and inflation be zero each. Step one refers to the supply shock. In terms of the model there is an increase in B of 2 units and an increase in A of equally 2 units. Step two refers to the outside lag. Inflation goes from zero to 2 percent. And unemployment goes from zero to 2 percent as well. Step three refers to the policy response. What is needed, according to the model, is to hold money supply constant. Step four refers to the outside lag. Obviously, inflation stays at 2 percent, and unemployment stays at 2 percent as well. Table 1.4 gives an overview.

As a result, given a supply shock, monetary policy is ineffective. The supply shock causes a loss of 8 units. However, monetary policy cannot reduce the loss.

Table 1.4
Monetary Policy in Europe
A Supply Shock

Unemployment	0	Inflation	0
Shock in A	2	Shock in B	2
Unemployment	2	Inflation	2
Change in Money Supply	0		
Unemployment	2	Inflation	2

3) A mixed shock in Europe. Let initial unemployment and inflation be zero each. Step one refers to the mixed shock. In terms of the model there is an increase in B of 2 units. Step two refers to the outside lag. Inflation goes from zero to 2 percent. And unemployment stays at zero percent. Step three refers to the policy response. What is needed, according to the model, is a reduction in money supply of 1 unit. Step four refers to the outside lag. Inflation goes from 2 to 1 percent. And unemployment goes from zero to 1 percent. For a synopsis see Table 1.5.

As a result, given a mixed shock, monetary policy can reduce the loss caused by inflation and unemployment. However, it cannot achieve zero inflation and zero unemployment. The mixed shock causes a loss of 4 units. Then monetary policy can reduce the loss to 2 units.

4) Another mixed shock in Europe. Let initial unemployment and inflation be zero each. Step one refers to the mixed shock. In terms of the model there is an increase in A of 2 units. Step two refers to the outside lag. Unemployment goes from zero to 2 percent. And inflation stays at zero percent. Step three refers to the policy response. What is needed, according to the model, is an increase in money

supply of 1 unit. Step four refers to the outside lag. Unemployment goes from 2 to 1 percent. And inflation goes from zero to 1 percent. For an overview see Table 1.6.

As a result, given a mixed shock, monetary policy can reduce the loss caused by inflation and unemployment to a certain extent. The mixed shock causes a loss of 4 units. Then monetary policy can reduce the loss to 2 units.

Table 1.5
Monetary Policy in Europe
A Mixed Shock

Unemployment	0	Inflation	0
Shock in A	0	Shock in B	2
Unemployment	0	Inflation	2
Change in Money Supply	− 1		
Unemployment	1	Inflation	1

Table 1.6
Monetary Policy in Europe
Another Mixed Shock

Unemployment	0	Inflation	0
Shock in A	2	Shock in B	0
Unemployment	2	Inflation	0
Change in Money Supply	1		
Unemployment	1	Inflation	1

5) Summary. Given a demand shock, monetary policy can achieve both zero inflation and zero unemployment. Given a supply shock, monetary policy is ineffective. Given a mixed shock, monetary policy can reduce the loss caused by inflation and unemployment. However, it cannot achieve zero inflation and zero unemployment.

6) Comparing cases A and B. As to the policy targets there are two distinct cases. In case A, by definition, the target of the central bank is zero inflation. In case B, by definition, the targets of the central bank are zero inflation and zero unemployment. First consider a demand shock. In case A, given a demand shock, monetary policy can achieve zero inflation. And what is more, as a side effect, it can achieve zero unemployment. In case B, given a demand shock, monetary policy can achieve both zero inflation and zero unemployment. Second consider a supply shock. In case A, given a supply shock, monetary policy can achieve zero inflation. However, as a side effect, it causes an increase in unemployment. In case B, given a supply shock, monetary policy is ineffective.

Chapter 3
Fiscal Policy A

1. The Model

An increase in European government purchases lowers unemployment in Europe. On the other hand, it raises inflation there. In the numerical example, a unit increase in government purchases lowers the rate of unemployment by 1 percentage point. On the other hand, it raises the rate of inflation by 1 percentage point. For instance, let initial unemployment be 2 percent, and let initial inflation be 2 percent as well. Now consider a unit increase in government purchases. Then unemployment goes from 2 to 1 percent. On the other hand, inflation goes from 2 to 3 percent.

The model of unemployment and inflation can be represented by a system of two equations:

$$u = A - \beta G \tag{1}$$

$$\pi = B + \beta\varepsilon G \tag{2}$$

Of course this is a reduced form. Here u denotes the rate of unemployment in Europe, π is the rate of inflation in Europe, G is European government purchases, β is the fiscal policy multiplier with respect to unemployment, $\beta\varepsilon$ is the fiscal policy multiplier with respect to inflation, A is some other factors bearing on the rate of unemployment in Europe, and B is some other factors bearing on the rate of inflation in Europe. The endogenous variables are the rate of unemployment and the rate of inflation in Europe.

According to equation (1), the rate of unemployment in Europe is a positive function of A and a negative function of European government purchases. According to equation (2), the rate of inflation in Europe is a positive function of B and a positive function of European government purchases. A unit increase in A raises the rate of unemployment by 1 percentage point. A unit increase in B

raises the rate of inflation by 1 percentage point. A unit increase in government purchases lowers the rate of unemployment by β percentage points. On the other hand, it raises the rate of inflation by $\beta\varepsilon$ percentage points.

As to policy targets there are two distinct cases. In case A the target of the government is zero unemployment. In case B the targets of the government are zero unemployment and zero inflation. This chapter deals with case A, and the next chapter deals with case B.

The target of the European government is zero unemployment in Europe. The instrument of the European government is European government purchases. By equation (1), the optimum level of European government purchases is:

$$G = \frac{A}{\beta} \tag{3}$$

That is, an increase in A requires an increase in European government purchases. And an increase in B requires no change in European government purchases. From equations (1) and (3) follows the optimum rate of unemployment in Europe:

$$u = 0 \tag{4}$$

And from equations (2) and (3) follows the optimum rate of inflation in Europe:

$$\pi = \varepsilon A + B \tag{5}$$

Unemployment in Europe is zero. By contrast, inflation there is not zero.

2. Some Numerical Examples

For ease of exposition we assume that fiscal policy multipliers are unity $\beta = \varepsilon = 1$. On this assumption, the model of unemployment and inflation can be written as follows:

$$u = A - G \tag{1}$$
$$\pi = B + G \tag{2}$$

A unit increase in A raises the rate of unemployment by 1 percentage point. A unit increase in B raises the rate of inflation by 1 percentage point. A unit increase in government purchases lowers the rate of unemployment by 1 percentage point. On the other hand, it raises the rate of inflation by 1 percentage point. The model can be solved this way:

$$G = A \tag{3}$$
$$u = 0 \tag{4}$$
$$\pi = A + B \tag{5}$$

Equation (3) shows the optimum level of government purchases, equation (4) shows the optimum rate of unemployment, and equation (5) shows the optimum rate of inflation.

It proves useful to study two distinct cases:
- a demand shock in Europe
- a supply shock in Europe.

1) A demand shock in Europe. Let initial unemployment be zero, and let initial inflation be zero as well. Step one refers to a decline in aggregate demand. In terms of the model there is an increase in A of 2 units and a decline in B of equally 2 units. Step two refers to the outside lag. Unemployment goes from zero to 2 percent. And inflation goes from zero to –2 percent. Step three refers to the policy response. What is needed, according to the model, is an increase in

government purchases of 2 units. Step four refers to the outside lag. Unemployment goes from 2 to zero percent. And inflation goes from −2 to zero percent. Table 1.7 presents a synopsis.

As a result, given a demand shock, fiscal policy can achieve zero unemployment. And what is more, as a side effect, it can achieve zero inflation. The loss function of the government is:

$$L_2 = u^2 \qquad (6)$$

The initial loss is zero. The demand shock causes a loss of 4 units. Then fiscal policy can reduce the loss to zero.

2) A supply shock in Europe. Let initial unemployment and inflation be zero each. Step one refers to the supply shock. In terms of the model there is an increase in B of 2 units and an increase in A of equally 2 units. Step two refers to the outside lag. Inflation goes from zero to 2 percent. And unemployment goes from zero to 2 percent as well. Step three refers to the policy response. What is needed, according to the model, is an increase in government purchases of 2 units. Step four refers to the outside lag. Unemployment goes from 2 to zero percent. And inflation goes from 2 to 4 percent. Table 1.8 gives an overview.

As a result, given a supply shock, fiscal policy can achieve zero unemployment. However, as a side effect, it causes an increase in inflation. The supply shock causes a loss of 4 units. Then fiscal policy can reduce the loss to zero.

3) Summary. Given a demand shock, fiscal policy can achieve zero unemployment. And what is more, as a side effect, it can achieve zero inflation. Given a supply shock, fiscal policy can achieve zero unemployment. However, as a side effect, it causes an increase in inflation.

Table 1.7
Fiscal Policy in Europe
A Demand Shock

Unemployment	0	Inflation	0
Shock in A	2	Shock in B	−2
Unemployment	2	Inflation	−2
Change in Govt Purchases	2		
Unemployment	0	Inflation	0

Table 1.8
Fiscal Policy in Europe
A Supply Shock

Unemployment	0	Inflation	0
Shock in A	2	Shock in B	2
Unemployment	2	Inflation	2
Change in Govt Purchases	2		
Unemployment	0	Inflation	4

Chapter 4
Fiscal Policy B

1. The Model

The model of unemployment and inflation can be characterized by a system of two equations:

$$u = A - \beta G \tag{1}$$

$$\pi = B + \beta \varepsilon G \tag{2}$$

The targets of the European government are zero unemployment and zero inflation in Europe. The instrument of the European government is European government purchases. There are two targets but only one instrument, so what is needed is a loss function. We assume that the European government has a quadratic loss function:

$$L_2 = \pi^2 + u^2 \tag{3}$$

L_2 is the loss to the European government caused by inflation and unemployment. For ease of exposition we assume equal weights in the loss function. The specific target of the European government is to minimize the loss, given the inflation function and the unemployment function. Taking account of equations (1) and (2), the loss function of the European government can be written as follows:

$$L_2 = (B + \beta \varepsilon G)^2 + (A - \beta G)^2 \tag{4}$$

Then the first-order condition for a minimum loss is:

$$G = \frac{A - \varepsilon B}{\beta + \beta \varepsilon^2} \tag{5}$$

Here G is the optimum level of European government purchases. An increase in A requires an increase in European government purchases. And an increase in B requires a cut in European government purchases. From equations (1) and (5) follows the optimum rate of unemployment in Europe:

$$u = \frac{\varepsilon^2 A + \varepsilon B}{1 + \varepsilon^2} \tag{6}$$

And from equations (2) and (5) follows the optimum rate of inflation in Europe:

$$\pi = \frac{\varepsilon A + B}{1 + \varepsilon^2} \tag{7}$$

The comparison of equations (6) and (7) gives:

$$u = \varepsilon \pi \tag{8}$$

Unemployment in Europe is not zero, nor is inflation there.

2. Some Numerical Examples

We assume that fiscal policy multipliers are unity $\beta = \varepsilon = 1$. On this assumption, the model of unemployment and inflation can be written as follows:

$$u = A - G \tag{1}$$
$$\pi = B + G \tag{2}$$

A unit increase in government purchases lowers the rate of unemployment by 1 percentage point. On the other hand, it raises the rate of inflation by 1 percentage point. The model can be solved this way:

$$2G = A - B \tag{3}$$
$$2u = A + B \tag{4}$$
$$2\pi = A + B \tag{5}$$

Equation (3) shows the optimum level of government purchases, equation (4) shows the optimum rate of unemployment, and equation (5) shows the optimum rate of inflation.

It proves useful to study two distinct cases:
- a demand shock in Europe
- a supply shock in Europe.

1) A demand shock in Europe. Let initial unemployment be zero, and let initial inflation be zero as well. Step one refers to a decline in aggregate demand. In terms of the model there is an increase in A of 2 units and a decline in B of equally 2 units. Step two refers to the outside lag. Unemployment goes from zero to 2 percent. And inflation goes from zero to –2 percent. Step three refers to the policy response. What is needed, according to the model, is an increase in government purchases of 2 units. Step four refers to the outside lag. Unemployment goes from 2 to zero percent. And inflation goes from –2 to zero percent. Table 1.9 presents a synopsis.

As a result, given a demand shock, fiscal policy can achieve both zero unemployment and zero inflation. The loss function of the government is:

$$L_2 = \pi^2 + u^2 \tag{6}$$

The initial loss is zero. The demand shock causes a loss of 8 units. Then fiscal policy can reduce the loss to zero.

Table 1.9
Fiscal Policy in Europe
A Demand Shock

Unemployment	0	Inflation	0
Shock in A	2	Shock in B	− 2
Unemployment	2	Inflation	− 2
Change in Govt Purchases	2		
Unemployment	0	Inflation	0

2) A supply shock in Europe. Let initial unemployment and inflation be zero each. Step one refers to the supply shock. In terms of the model there is an increase in B of 2 units and an increase in A of equally 2 units. Step two refers to the outside lag. Inflation goes from zero to 2 percent. And unemployment goes from zero to 2 percent as well. Step three refers to the policy response. What is needed, according to the model, is to hold government purchases constant. Step four refers to the outside lag. Obviously, inflation stays at 2 percent, and unemployment stays at 2 percent as well. Table 1.10 gives an overview.

As a result, given a supply shock, fiscal policy is ineffective. The supply shock causes a loss of 8 units. However, fiscal policy cannot reduce the loss.

Table 1.10
Fiscal Policy in Europe
A Supply Shock

Unemployment	0	Inflation	0
Shock in A	2	Shock in B	2
Unemployment	2	Inflation	2
Change in Govt Purchases	0		
Unemployment	2	Inflation	2

3) Summary. Given a demand shock, fiscal policy can achieve both zero unemployment and zero inflation. Given a supply shock, fiscal policy is ineffective. Given a mixed shock, fiscal policy can reduce the loss caused by unemployment and inflation. However, it cannot achieve zero unemployment and zero inflation.

4) Comparing cases A and B. As to the policy targets there are two distinct cases. In case A, by definition, the target of the government is zero unemployment. In case B, by definition, the targets of the government are zero unemployment and zero inflation. First consider a demand shock. In case A, given a demand shock, fiscal policy can achieve zero unemployment. And what is more, as a side effect, it can achieve zero inflation. In case B, given a demand shock, fiscal policy can achieve both zero unemployment and zero inflation. Second consider a supply shock. In case A, given a supply shock, fiscal policy can achieve zero unemployment. However, as a side effect, it causes an increase in inflation. In case B, given a supply shock, fiscal policy is ineffective.

Chapter 5
Interaction between
Central Bank and Government

An increase in European money supply lowers unemployment in Europe. On the other hand, it raises inflation there. Correspondingly, an increase in European government purchases lowers unemployment in Europe. On the other hand, it raises inflation there. The primary target of the European central bank is zero inflation in Europe. By contrast, the primary target of the European government is zero unemployment there.

The model of unemployment and inflation can be represented by a system of two equations:

$$u = A - \alpha M - \beta G \tag{1}$$

$$\pi = B + \alpha \varepsilon M + \beta \varepsilon G \tag{2}$$

Of course this is a reduced form. Here u denotes the rate of unemployment in Europe, π is the rate of inflation in Europe, M is European money supply, G is European government purchases, α is the monetary policy multiplier with respect to unemployment, $\alpha\varepsilon$ is the monetary policy multiplier with respect to inflation, β is the fiscal policy multiplier with respect to unemployment, $\beta\varepsilon$ is the fiscal policy multiplier with respect to inflation, A is some other factors bearing on the rate of unemployment in Europe, and B is some other factors bearing on the rate of inflation in Europe. The endogenous variables are the rate of unemployment and the rate of inflation in Europe.

According to equation (1), the rate of unemployment in Europe is a positive function of A, a negative function of European money supply, and a negative function of European government purchases. According to equation (2), the rate of inflation in Europe is a positive function of B, a positive function of European money supply, and a positive function of European government purchases. A unit increase in A raises the rate of unemployment by 1 percentage point. A unit increase in B raises the rate of inflation by 1 percentage point. A unit increase in money supply lowers the rate of unemployment by α percentage points. On the other hand, it raises the rate of inflation by $\alpha\varepsilon$ percentage points. A unit increase in government purchases lowers the rate of unemployment by β percentage points. On the other hand, it raises the rate of inflation by $\beta\varepsilon$ percentage points.

As to policy targets there are three distinct cases. In case A the target of the central bank is zero inflation. And the target of the government is zero unemployment. In case B the targets of the central bank are zero inflation and zero unemployment. And the target of the government still is zero unemployment. In case C the targets of the central bank are zero inflation and zero unemployment. And the targets of the government are zero unemployment and zero inflation.

1) Case A. The target of the European central bank is zero inflation in Europe. The instrument of the European central bank is European money supply. By equation (2), the reaction function of the European central bank is:

$$\alpha\varepsilon M = -B - \beta\varepsilon G \tag{3}$$

Suppose the European government raises European government purchases. Then, as a response, the European central bank lowers European money supply.

The target of the European government is zero unemployment in Europe. The instrument of the European government is European government purchases. By equation (1), the reaction function of the European government is:

$$\beta G = A - \alpha M \tag{4}$$

Suppose the European central bank lowers European money supply. Then, as a response, the European government raises European government purchases.

The Nash equilibrium is determined by the reaction functions of the European central bank and the European government. From the reaction function of the European central bank follows:

$$\frac{dM}{dG} = -\frac{\beta}{\alpha} \qquad (5)$$

And from the reaction function of the European government follows:

$$\frac{dG}{dM} = -\frac{\alpha}{\beta} \qquad (6)$$

That is to say, the reaction curves do not intersect. As an important result, in case A there is no Nash equilibrium.

2) Case B. The targets of the European central bank are zero inflation and zero unemployment in Europe. The instrument of the European central bank is European money supply. There are two targets but only one instrument, so what is needed is a loss function. We assume that the European central bank has a quadratic loss function:

$$L_1 = \pi^2 + u^2 \qquad (7)$$

L_1 is the loss to the European central bank caused by inflation and unemployment. For ease of exposition we assume equal weights in the loss function. The specific target of the European central bank is to minimize the loss, given the inflation function and the unemployment function. Taking account of equations (1) and (2), the loss function of the European central bank can be written as follows:

$$L_1 = (B + \alpha\varepsilon M + \beta\varepsilon G)^2 + (A - \alpha M - \beta G)^2 \qquad (8)$$

Then the first-order condition for a minimum loss gives the reaction function of the European central bank:

$$(1+\varepsilon^2)\alpha M = A - \varepsilon B - (1+\varepsilon^2)\beta G \qquad (9)$$

Suppose the European government raises European government purchases. Then, as a response, the European central bank lowers European money supply.

The target of the European government is zero unemployment in Europe. The instrument of the European government is European government purchases. By equation (1), the reaction function of the European government is:

$$\beta G = A - \alpha M \tag{10}$$

Suppose the European central bank lowers European money supply. Then, as a response, the European government raises European government purchases.

The Nash equilibrium is determined by the reaction functions of the European central bank and the European government. From the reaction function of the European central bank follows:

$$\frac{dM}{dG} = -\frac{\beta}{\alpha} \tag{11}$$

And from the reaction function of the European government follows:

$$\frac{dG}{dM} = -\frac{\alpha}{\beta} \tag{12}$$

That is to say, the reaction curves do not intersect. As an important result, in case B there is no Nash equilibrium.

3) Case C. The targets of the European central bank are zero inflation and zero unemployment in Europe. The instrument of the European central bank is European money supply. There are two targets but only one instrument, so what is needed is a loss function. We assume that the European central bank has a quadratic loss function:

$$L_1 = \pi^2 + u^2 \tag{13}$$

L_1 is the loss to the European central bank caused by inflation and unemployment. We assume equal weights in the loss function. The specific target of the European central bank is to minimize the loss, given the inflation function and the unemployment function. Taking account of equations (1) and (2), the loss function of the European central bank can be written as follows:

$$L_1 = (B + \alpha\varepsilon M + \beta\varepsilon G)^2 + (A - \alpha M - \beta G)^2 \tag{14}$$

Then the first-order condition for a minimum loss gives the reaction function of the European central bank:

$$(1+\varepsilon^2)\alpha M = A - \varepsilon B - (1+\varepsilon^2)\beta G \tag{15}$$

Suppose the European government raises European government purchases. Then, as a response, the European central bank lowers European money supply.

The targets of the European government are zero unemployment and zero inflation in Europe. The instrument of the European government is European government purchases. There are two targets but only one instrument, so what is needed is a loss function. We assume that the European government has a quadratic loss function:

$$L_2 = \pi^2 + u^2 \tag{16}$$

L_2 is the loss to the European government caused by inflation and unemployment. We assume equal weights in the loss function. The specific target of the European government is to minimize the loss, given the inflation function and the unemployment function. Taking account of equations (1) and (2), the loss function of the European government can be written as follows:

$$L_2 = (B + \alpha\varepsilon M + \beta\varepsilon G)^2 + (A - \alpha M - \beta G)^2 \tag{17}$$

Then the first-order condition for a minimum loss gives the reaction function of the European government:

$$(1+\varepsilon^2)\beta G = A - \varepsilon B - (1+\varepsilon^2)\alpha M \tag{18}$$

Suppose the European central bank lowers European money supply. Then, as a response, the European government raises European government purchases.

The Nash equilibrium is determined by the reaction functions of the European central bank and the European government. Obviously, equations (15) and (18) are identical. There are two endogenous variables, European money supply and European government purchases. On the other hand, there is only one independent equation. As an important result, in case C there are multiple Nash equilibria.

4) Summary. In case A there is no Nash equilibrium. In case B there is no Nash equilibrium either. And in case C there are multiple Nash equilibria.

Chapter 6
Cooperation between
Central Bank and Government

1. The Model

An increase in European money supply lowers unemployment in Europe. On the other hand, it raises inflation there. Correspondingly, an increase in European government purchases lowers unemployment in Europe. On the other hand, it raises inflation there. The policy makers are the European central bank and the European government. The targets of policy cooperation are zero inflation and zero unemployment in Europe.

The model of unemployment and inflation can be characterized by a system of two equations:

$$u = A - \alpha M - \beta G \tag{1}$$

$$\pi = B + \alpha\varepsilon M + \beta\varepsilon G \tag{2}$$

Of course this is a reduced form. Here u denotes the rate of unemployment in Europe, π is the rate of inflation in Europe, M is European money supply, G is European government purchases, α is the monetary policy multiplier with respect to unemployment, $\alpha\varepsilon$ is the monetary policy multiplier with respect to inflation, β is the fiscal policy multiplier with respect to unemployment, $\beta\varepsilon$ is the fiscal policy multiplier with respect to inflation, A is some other factors bearing on the rate of unemployment in Europe, and B is some other factors bearing on the rate of inflation in Europe. The endogenous variables are the rate of unemployment and the rate of inflation in Europe.

According to equation (1), the rate of unemployment in Europe is a positive function of A, a negative function of European money supply, and a negative function of European government purchases. According to equation (2), the rate of inflation in Europe is a positive function of B, a positive function of European

M. Carlberg et al., *Strategic Policy Interactions in a Monetary Union*,
DOI: 10.1007/978-3-540-92751-8_7, © Springer-Verlag Berlin Heidelberg 2009

money supply, and a positive function of European government purchases. A unit increase in A raises the rate of unemployment by 1 percentage point. A unit increase in B raises the rate of inflation by 1 percentage point. A unit increase in money supply lowers the rate of unemployment by α percentage points. On the other hand, it raises the rate of inflation by $\alpha\varepsilon$ percentage points. A unit increase in government purchases lowers the rate of unemployment by β percentage points. On the other hand, it raises the rate of inflation by $\beta\varepsilon$ percentage points.

The policy makers are the European central bank and the European government. The targets of policy cooperation are zero inflation and zero unemployment in Europe. The instruments of policy cooperation are European money supply and European government purchases. Thus there are two targets and two instruments. We assume that the policy makers agree on a common loss function:

$$L = \pi^2 + u^2 \qquad (3)$$

L is the loss caused by inflation and unemployment. For ease of exposition we assume equal weights in the loss function. The specific target of policy cooperation is to minimize the loss, given the inflation function and the unemployment function. Taking account of equations (1) and (2), the loss function under policy cooperation can be written as follows:

$$L = (B + \alpha\varepsilon M + \beta\varepsilon G)^2 + (A - \alpha M - \beta G)^2 \qquad (4)$$

Then the first-order conditions for a minimum loss are:

$$(1+\varepsilon^2)\alpha M = A - \varepsilon B - (1+\varepsilon^2)\beta G \qquad (5)$$

$$(1+\varepsilon^2)\beta G = A - \varepsilon B - (1+\varepsilon^2)\alpha M \qquad (6)$$

Equation (5) shows the first-order condition with respect to European money supply. And equation (6) shows the first-order condition with respect to European government purchases. Obviously, equations (5) and (6) are identical. There are two endogenous variables, European money supply and European government purchases. On the other hand, there is only one independent equation. Thus there is an infinite number of solutions.

The cooperative equilibrium is determined by the first-order conditions for a minimum loss:

$$\alpha M + \beta G = \frac{A - \varepsilon B}{1 + \varepsilon^2} \tag{7}$$

Equation (7) yields the optimum combinations of European money supply and European government purchases. As a result, monetary and fiscal cooperation can reduce the loss caused by inflation and unemployment.

From equations (1) and (7) follows the optimum rate of unemployment in Europe:

$$u = \frac{\varepsilon^2 A + \varepsilon B}{1 + \varepsilon^2} \tag{8}$$

And from equations (2) and (7) follows the optimum rate of inflation in Europe:

$$\pi = \frac{\varepsilon A + B}{1 + \varepsilon^2} \tag{9}$$

Unemployment in Europe is not zero, nor is inflation there.

2. Some Numerical Examples

For ease of exposition we assume that monetary and fiscal policy multipliers are unity $\alpha = \beta = \varepsilon = 1$. On this assumption, the model of unemployment and inflation can be written as follows:

$$u = A - M - G \tag{1}$$

$$\pi = B + M + G \tag{2}$$

A unit increase in A raises the rate of unemployment by 1 percentage point. A unit increase in B raises the rate of inflation by 1 percentage point. A unit increase in money supply lowers the rate of unemployment by 1 percentage point. On the other hand, it raises the rate of inflation by 1 percentage point. A unit increase in government purchases lowers the rate of unemployment by 1 percentage point. On the other hand, it raises the rate of inflation by 1 percentage point. The model can be solved this way:

$$2M + 2G = A - B \tag{3}$$

$$2u = A + B \tag{4}$$

$$2\pi = A + B \tag{5}$$

Equation (3) shows the optimum combinations of money supply and government purchases, equation (4) shows the optimum rate of unemployment, and equation (5) shows the optimum rate of inflation.

It proves useful to study three distinct cases:
- a demand shock in Europe
- a supply shock in Europe
- a mixed shock in Europe.

1) A demand shock in Europe. Let initial unemployment be zero, and let initial inflation be zero as well. Step one refers to a decline in aggregate demand. In terms of the model there is an increase in A of 2 units and a decline in B of

equally 2 units. Step two refers to the outside lag. Unemployment goes from zero to 2 percent. And inflation goes from zero to –2 percent. Step three refers to the policy response. According to the model, a first solution is an increase in money supply of 2 units and an increase in government purchases of zero units. Step four refers to the outside lag. Unemployment goes from 2 to zero percent. And inflation goes from –2 to zero percent. Table 1.11 presents a synopsis.

As a result, given a demand shock, monetary and fiscal cooperation can achieve both zero inflation and zero unemployment. A second solution is an increase in money supply of 1 unit and an increase in government purchases of equally 1 unit. A third solution is an increase in money supply of zero units and an increase in government purchases of 2 units. And so on. The loss function under policy cooperation is:

$$L = \pi^2 + u^2 \qquad (6)$$

The initial loss is zero. The demand shock causes a loss of 8 units. Then policy cooperation can reduce the loss to zero.

Table 1.11
Cooperation between Central Bank and Government
A Demand Shock

Unemployment	0	Inflation	0
Shock in A	2	Shock in B	– 2
Unemployment	2	Inflation	– 2
Change in Money Supply	2	Change in Govt Purchases	0
Unemployment	0	Inflation	0

2) A supply shock in Europe. Let initial unemployment and inflation be zero each. Step one refers to the supply shock. In terms of the model there is an

increase in B of 2 units and an increase in A of equally 2 units. Step two refers to the outside lag. Inflation goes from zero to 2 percent. And unemployment goes from zero to 2 percent as well. Step three refers to the policy response. According to the model, a first solution is to keep money supply and government purchases constant. Step four refers to the outside lag. Obviously, inflation stays at 2 percent, and unemployment stays at 2 percent as well. Table 1.12 gives an overview.

As a result, given a supply shock, monetary and fiscal cooperation is ineffective. The supply shock causes a loss of 8 units. However, policy cooperation cannot reduce the loss.

Table 1.12
Cooperation between Central Bank and Government
A Supply Shock

Unemployment	0	Inflation	0
Shock in A	2	Shock in B	2
Unemployment	2	Inflation	2
Change in Money Supply	0	Change in Govt Purchases	0
Unemployment	2	Inflation	2

3) A mixed shock in Europe. Let initial unemployment and inflation be zero each. Step one refers to the mixed shock. In terms of the model there is an increase in B of 4 units. Step two refers to the outside lag. Inflation goes from zero to 4 percent. And unemployment stays at zero percent. Step three refers to the policy response. According to the model, a first solution is a reduction in money supply of 2 units and a reduction in government purchases of zero units. Step four refers to the outside lag. Inflation goes from 4 to 2 percent. And unemployment goes from zero to 2 percent. For a synopsis see Table 1.13.

As a result, given a mixed shock, monetary and fiscal cooperation can reduce the loss caused by inflation and unemployment. However, it cannot achieve zero inflation and zero unemployment. A second solution is a reduction in money supply of 1 unit and a reduction in government purchases of equally 1 unit. A third solution is a reduction in money supply of zero units and a reduction in government purchases of 2 units. And so on. The mixed shock causes a loss of 16 units. Then policy cooperation can reduce the loss to 8 units.

Table 1.13
Cooperation between Central Bank and Government
A Mixed Shock

Unemployment	0	Inflation	0
Shock in A	0	Shock in B	4
Unemployment	0	Inflation	4
Change in Money Supply	−2	Change in Govt Purchases	0
Unemployment	2	Inflation	2

4) Summary. Given a demand shock, policy cooperation can achieve both zero inflation and zero unemployment. Given a supply shock, policy cooperation is ineffective. Given a mixed shock, policy cooperation can reduce the loss caused by inflation and unemployment to a certain extent.

5) Comparing policy cooperation with policy interaction. Under policy interaction there is no unique Nash equilibrium. By contrast, policy cooperation can reduce the loss caused by inflation and unemployment. Judging from this point of view, policy cooperation seems to be superior to policy interaction.

Chapter 7
Interaction between Central Bank and Government: A Special Case

1. The Model

The model of unemployment and inflation can be represented by a system of two equations:

$$u = A - \alpha M - \beta G \tag{1}$$

$$\pi = B + \gamma M + \delta G \tag{2}$$

Here α denotes the monetary policy multiplier with respect to unemployment, β is the fiscal policy multiplier with respect to unemployment, γ is the monetary policy multiplier with respect to inflation, and δ is the fiscal policy multiplier with respect to inflation.

According to equation (1), the rate of unemployment in Europe is a positive function of A, a negative function of European money supply, and a negative function of European government purchases. According to equation (2), the rate of inflation in Europe is a positive function of B, a positive function of European money supply, and a positive function of European government purchases. An increase in money supply lowers unemployment. On the other hand, it raises inflation. Correspondingly, an increase in government purchases lowers unemployment. On the other hand, it raises inflation. A unit increase in money supply lowers the rate of unemployment by α percentage points. On the other hand, it raises the rate of inflation by γ percentage points. A unit increase in government purchases lowers the rate of unemployment by β percentage points. On the other hand, it raises the rate of inflation by δ percentage points.

The target of the European central bank is zero inflation in Europe. The instrument of the European central bank is European money supply. By equation (2), the reaction function of the European central bank is:

$$\gamma M = -B - \delta G \tag{3}$$

Suppose the European government raises European government purchases. Then, as a response, the European central bank lowers European money supply.

The target of the European government is zero unemployment in Europe. The instrument of the European government is European government purchases. By equation (1), the reaction function of the European government is:

$$\beta G = A - \alpha M \tag{4}$$

Suppose the European central bank lowers European money supply. Then, as a response, the European government raises European government purchases.

The Nash equilibrium is determined by the reaction functions of the European central bank and the European government. The solution to this problem is as follows:

$$M = \frac{\delta A + \beta B}{\alpha \delta - \beta \gamma} \tag{5}$$

$$G = \frac{\gamma A + \alpha B}{\beta \gamma - \alpha \delta} \tag{6}$$

Equations (5) and (6) show the Nash equilibrium of European money supply and European government purchases. As a result, there is a unique Nash equilibrium.

2. Some Numerical Examples

We assume $\alpha = \beta = \gamma = 1$ and $\delta = 1.1$. On this assumption, the model of unemployment and inflation can be written as follows:

$$u = A - M - G \tag{1}$$

$$\pi = B + M + 1.1\,G \tag{2}$$

A unit increase in money supply lowers the rate of unemployment by 1 percentage point. On the other hand, it raises the rate of inflation by 1 percentage point. A unit increase in government purchases lowers the rate of unemployment by 1 percentage point. On the other hand, it raises the rate of inflation by 1.1 percentage points.

The Nash equilibrium can be described by two equations:

$$M = 11A + 10B \tag{3}$$

$$G = -10A - 10B \tag{4}$$

Equations (3) and (4) show the equilibrium levels of money supply and government purchases. An increase in A causes an increase in money supply and a cut in government purchases. And the same in true of an increase in B. To be more specific, a unit increase in A causes an increase in money supply of 11 units and a cut in government purchases of 10 units. A unit increase in B causes an increase in money supply of 10 units and a cut in government purchases of equally 10 units.

It proves useful to study three distinct cases:
- a demand shock in Europe
- a supply shock in Europe
- a mixed shock in Europe.

1) A demand shock in Europe. Let initial unemployment be zero, and let initial inflation be zero as well. Step one refers to a decline in aggregate demand. In terms of the model there is an increase in A of 1 unit and a decline in B of equally 1 unit. Step two refers to the outside lag. Unemployment goes from zero to 1 percent. And inflation goes from zero to −1 percent. Step three refers to the policy response. According to the Nash equilibrium there is an increase in money supply of 1 unit and an increase in government purchases of zero units. Step four refers to the outside lag. Unemployment goes from 1 to zero percent. And inflation goes from −1 to zero percent. Table 1.14 presents a synopsis.

Table 1.14
Interaction between Central Bank and Government
A Demand Shock

Unemployment	0	Inflation	0
Shock in A	1	Shock in B	−1
Unemployment	1	Inflation	−1
Change in Money Supply	1	Change in Govt Purchases	0
Unemployment	0	Inflation	0

As a result, given a demand shock, monetary and fiscal interaction can achieve both zero inflation and zero unemployment. And what is more, the required change in money supply is small. The loss functions of the central bank and the government are respectively:

$$L_1 = \pi^2 \tag{5}$$
$$L_2 = u^2 \tag{6}$$

The initial loss of the central bank is zero, as is the initial loss of the government. The demand shock causes a loss to the central bank of 1 unit and a loss to the government of equally 1 unit. Then policy interaction can reduce the loss of the central bank and the government to zero each.

2) A supply shock in Europe. Let initial unemployment and inflation be zero each. Step one refers to the supply shock. In terms of the model there is an increase in B of 1 unit and an increase in A of equally 1 unit. Step two refers to the outside lag. Inflation goes from zero to 1 percent. And unemployment goes from zero to 1 percent as well. Step three refers to the policy response. According to the Nash equilibrium there is an increase in money supply of 21 units and a reduction in government purchases of 20 units. Step four refers to the outside lag. Inflation goes from 1 to zero percent. And unemployment goes from 1 to zero percent as well. Table 1.15 gives an overview.

As a result, given a supply shock, monetary and fiscal interaction can achieve both zero inflation and zero unemployment. However, the required increase in money supply is extremely large. And the same holds for the required cut in government purchases. This solution does not make much sense.

3) A mixed shock in Europe. Let initial unemployment and inflation be zero each. Step one refers to the mixed shock. In terms of the model there is an increase in B of 1 unit. Step two refers to the outside lag. Inflation goes from zero to 1 percent. And unemployment stays at zero percent. Step three refers to the policy response. According to the Nash equilibrium there is an increase in money supply of 10 units and a reduction in government purchases of equally 10 units. Step four refers to the outside lag. Inflation goes from 1 to zero percent. And unemployment stays at zero percent. For a synopsis see Table 1.16.

As a result, given a mixed shock, monetary and fiscal interaction can achieve both zero inflation and zero unemployment. However, the required increase in money supply is extremely large. And the same applies to the required cut in government purchases. This solution is not convincing.

4) Summary. Given a demand shock, policy interaction can achieve zero inflation and zero unemployment. And what is more, the required change in money supply is small. Given a supply shock, policy interaction can achieve zero inflation and zero unemployment. However, the required increase in money supply is extremely large. And the same is true of the required cut in government

purchases. This solution does not make much sense. Given a mixed shock, policy interaction can achieve zero inflation and zero unemployment. However, the required increase in money supply is extremely large. And the same applies to the required cut in government purchases. This solution is not convincing.

Table 1.15
Interaction between Central Bank and Government
A Supply Shock

Unemployment	0	Inflation	0
Shock in A	1	Shock in B	1
Unemployment	1	Inflation	1
Change in Money Supply	21	Change in Govt Purchases	− 20
Unemployment	0	Inflation	0

Table 1.16
Interaction between Central Bank and Government
A Mixed Shock

Unemployment	0	Inflation	0
Shock in A	0	Shock in B	1
Unemployment	0	Inflation	1
Change in Money Supply	10	Change in Govt Purchases	− 10
Unemployment	0	Inflation	0

Part Two

The Monetary Union as a Whole

Presence of a Deficit Target

Chapter 1
Fiscal Policy A

1. The Model

An increase in European government purchases lowers unemployment in Europe. On the other hand, it raises inflation there. And what is more, it raises the structural deficit.

The model of unemployment, inflation, and the structural deficit can be represented by a system of three equations:

$$u = \frac{A-G}{\overline{Y}} \tag{1}$$

$$\pi = \frac{B+G}{\overline{Y}} \tag{2}$$

$$s = \frac{G-T}{\overline{Y}} \tag{3}$$

Here u denotes the rate of unemployment in Europe, π is the rate of inflation in Europe, s is the structural deficit ratio in Europe, G is European government purchases, T is European tax revenue at full-employment output, $G-T$ is the structural deficit in Europe, A is some other factors bearing on the rate of unemployment in Europe, B is some other factors bearing on the rate of inflation in Europe, and $\overline{Y}$ is full-employment output in Europe. The endogenous variables are the rate of unemployment, the rate of inflation, and the structural deficit ratio.

According to equation (1), the rate of unemployment in Europe is a positive function of A and a negative function of European government purchases. According to equation (2), the rate of inflation in Europe is a positive function of B and a positive function of European government purchases. According to equation (3), the structural deficit ratio in Europe is a positive function of European government purchases.

To simplify notation we assume that full-employment output in Europe is unity. On this assumption, the model can be written as follows:

$$u = A - G \tag{4}$$

$$\pi = B + G \tag{5}$$

$$s = G - T \tag{6}$$

A unit increase in government purchases lowers the rate of unemployment by 1 percentage point. On the other hand, it raises the rate of inflation by 1 percentage point. And what is more, it raises the structural deficit ratio by 1 percentage point. For instance, let initial unemployment be 2 percent, let initial inflation be 2 percent, and let the initial structural deficit be 2 percent as well. Now consider a unit increase in government purchases. Then unemployment goes from 2 to 1 percent. On the other hand, inflation goes from 2 to 3 percent. And what is more, the structural deficit goes from 2 to 3 percent as well.

As to policy targets there are two distinct cases. In case A the targets of the government are zero unemployment and a zero structural deficit. In case B the targets of the government are zero unemployment, zero inflation, and a zero structural deficit. This chapter deals with case A, and the next chapter deals with case B.

The targets of the European government are zero unemployment and a zero structural deficit in Europe. The instrument of the European government is European government purchases. There are two targets but only one instrument, so what is needed is a loss function. We assume that the European government has a quadratic loss function:

$$L_2 = u^2 + s^2 \tag{7}$$

L_2 is the loss to the European government caused by unemployment and the structural deficit. We assume equal weights in the loss function. The specific target of the European government is to minimize the loss, given the unemployment function and the structural deficit function. Taking account of equations (4) and (6), the loss function of the European government can be written as follows:

$$L_2 = (A - G)^2 + (G - T)^2 \tag{8}$$

Then the first-order condition for a minimum loss is:

$$2G = A + T \tag{9}$$

Here G is the optimum level of European government purchases. An increase in A requires an increase in European government purchases. And an increase in B requires no change in European government purchases. From equations (4) and (9) follows the optimum rate of unemployment in Europe:

$$2u = A - T \tag{10}$$

From equations (5) and (9) follows the optimum rate of inflation in Europe:

$$2\pi = A + 2B + T \tag{11}$$

And from equations (6) and (9) follows the optimum structural deficit ratio:

$$2s = A - T \tag{12}$$

Unemployment in Europe is not zero. And the same holds for inflation and the structural deficit there.

2. Some Numerical Examples

For easy reference, the basic model is summarized here:

$$u = A - G \tag{1}$$

$$\pi = B + G \tag{2}$$

$$s = G - T \tag{3}$$

And the optimum level of government purchases is:

$$2G = A + T \tag{4}$$

It proves useful to study two distinct cases:
- a demand shock in Europe
- a supply shock in Europe.

1) A demand shock in Europe. Let initial unemployment be zero, let initial inflation be zero, and let the initial structural deficit be zero as well. Step one refers to a decline in aggregate demand. In terms of the model there is an increase in A of 6 units and a decline in B of equally 6 units. Step two refers to the outside lag. Unemployment goes from zero to 6 percent. Inflation goes from zero to − 6 percent. And the structural deficit stays at zero percent. Step three refers to the policy response. What is needed, according to the model, is an increase in government purchases of 3 units. Step four refers to the outside lag. Unemployment goes from 6 to 3 percent. The structural deficit goes from zero to 3 percent. And inflation goes from − 6 to − 3 percent. Table 2.1 presents a synopsis.

As a result, given a demand shock, fiscal policy can reduce the loss caused by unemployment and the structural deficit. However, it cannot achieve zero unemployment and a zero structural deficit. The loss function of the government is:

$$L_2 = u^2 + s^2 \tag{5}$$

The initial loss is zero. The demand shock causes a loss of 36 units. Then fiscal policy can reduce the loss to 18 units.

Table 2.1
Fiscal Policy in Europe
A Demand Shock

Unemployment	0	Inflation	0
Structural Deficit	0		
Shock in A	6	Shock in B	− 6
Unemployment	6	Inflation	− 6
Structural Deficit	0		
Change in Govt Purchases	3		
Unemployment	3	Inflation	− 3
Structural Deficit	3		

2) A supply shock in Europe. Let initial unemployment be zero, let initial inflation be zero, and let the initial structural deficit be zero as well. Step one refers to the supply shock. In terms of the model there is an increase in B of 6 units and an increase in A of equally 6 units. Step two refers to the outside lag. Inflation goes from zero to 6 percent. Unemployment goes from zero to 6 percent as well. And the structural deficit stays at zero percent. Step three refers to the policy response. What is needed, according to the model, is an increase in government purchases of 3 units. Step four refers to the outside lag. Unemployment goes from 6 to 3 percent. The structural deficit goes from zero to 3 percent. And inflation goes from 6 to 9 percent. Table 2.2 gives an overview.

As a result, given a supply shock, fiscal policy can reduce the loss caused by unemployment and the structural deficit. However, it cannot achieve zero unemployment and a zero structural deficit. The supply shock causes a loss of 36 units. Then fiscal policy can reduce the loss to 18 units.

3) Summary. Given a demand shock, fiscal policy can reduce the loss to a certain extent. And the same is true of a supply shock.

Table 2.2
Fiscal Policy in Europe
A Supply Shock

Unemployment	0	Inflation	0
Structural Deficit	0		
Shock in A	6	Shock in B	6
Unemployment	6	Inflation	6
Structural Deficit	0		
Change in Govt Purchases	3		
Unemployment	3	Inflation	9
Structural Deficit	3		

Chapter 2
Fiscal Policy B

1. The Model

The model of unemployment, inflation, and the structural deficit can be characterized by a system of three equations:

$$u = A - G \tag{1}$$

$$\pi = B + G \tag{2}$$

$$s = G - T \tag{3}$$

The targets of the European government are zero unemployment, zero inflation, and a zero structural deficit. The instrument of the European government is European government purchases. There are three targets but only one instrument, so what is needed is a loss function. We assume that the European government has a quadratic loss function:

$$L_2 = \pi^2 + u^2 + s^2 \tag{4}$$

L_2 is the loss to the European government caused by inflation, unemployment, and the structural deficit. We assume equal weights in the loss function. The specific target of the European government is to minimize the loss, given the inflation function, the unemployment function, and the structural deficit function. Taking account of equations (1), (2) and (3), the loss function of the European government can be written as follows:

$$L_2 = (B+G)^2 + (A-G)^2 + (G-T)^2 \tag{5}$$

Then the first-order condition for a minimum loss is:

$$3G = A - B + T \tag{6}$$

Here G is the optimum level of European government purchases. An increase in A requires an increase in European government purchases. And an increase in B requires a cut in European government purchases. From equations (1) and (6) follows the optimum rate of unemployment in Europe:

$$3u = 2A + B - T \tag{7}$$

From equations (2) and (6) follows the optimum rate of inflation in Europe:

$$3\pi = A + 2B + T \tag{8}$$

And from equations (3) and (6) follows the optimum structural deficit ratio:

$$3s = A - B - 2T \tag{9}$$

Unemployment in Europe is not zero. And the same holds for inflation and the structural deficit there.

2. Some Numerical Examples

For easy reference, the basic model is reproduced here:

$$u = A - G \tag{1}$$
$$\pi = B + G \tag{2}$$
$$s = G - T \tag{3}$$

And the optimum level of government purchases is:

$$3G = A - B + T \tag{4}$$

It proves useful to study two distinct cases:
- a demand shock in Europe
- a supply shock in Europe.

1) A demand shock in Europe. Let initial unemployment be zero, let initial inflation be zero, and let the initial structural deficit be zero as well. Step one refers to a decline in aggregate demand. In terms of the model there is an increase in A of 6 units and a decline in B of equally 6 units. Step two refers to the outside lag. Unemployment goes from zero to 6 percent. Inflation goes from zero to − 6 percent. And the structural deficit stays at zero percent. Step three refers to the policy response. What is needed, according to the model, is an increase in government purchases of 4 units. Step four refers to the outside lag. Unemployment goes from 6 to 2 percent. Inflation goes from − 6 to − 2 percent. And the structural deficit goes from zero to 4 percent. Table 2.3 presents a synopsis.

Table 2.3
Fiscal Policy in Europe
A Demand Shock

Unemployment	0	Inflation	0
Structural Deficit	0		
Shock in A	6	Shock in B	− 6
Unemployment	6	Inflation	− 6
Structural Deficit	0		
Change in Govt Purchases	4		
Unemployment	2	Inflation	− 2
Structural Deficit	4		

As a result, given a demand shock, fiscal policy can reduce the loss caused by unemployment, inflation, and the structural deficit. However, it cannot achieve zero unemployment, zero inflation, and a zero structural deficit. The loss function of the government is:

$$L_2 = \pi^2 + u^2 + s^2 \tag{5}$$

The initial loss is zero. The demand shock causes a loss of 72 units. Then fiscal policy can reduce the loss to 24 units.

2) A supply shock in Europe. Let initial unemployment be zero, let initial inflation be zero, and let the initial structural deficit be zero as well. Step one refers to the supply shock. In terms of the model there is an increase in B of 6 units and an increase in A of equally 6 units. Step two refers to the outside lag. Inflation goes from zero to 6 percent. Unemployment goes from zero to 6 percent as well. And the structural deficit stays at zero percent. Step three refers to the policy response. What is needed, according to the model, is to hold government purchases constant. Step four refers to the outside lag. Obviously, inflation stays at 6 percent, unemployment stays at 6 percent, and the structural deficit stays at zero percent. Table 2.4 gives an overview.

As a result, given a supply shock, fiscal policy is ineffective. The supply shock causes a loss of 72 units. However, fiscal policy cannot reduce the loss.

3) Summary. Given a demand shock, fiscal policy can reduce the loss to a certain extent. Given a supply shock, fiscal policy is ineffective.

4) Comparing cases A and B. As to the policy targets there are two distinct cases. In case A, by definition, the targets of the government are zero unemployment and a zero structural deficit. In case B, by definition, the targets of the government are zero unemployment, zero inflation, and a zero structural deficit. First consider a demand shock. In case A, given a demand shock, fiscal policy can reduce the loss to a certain extent. In case B, given a demand shock, fiscal policy can reduce the loss to a greater extent. Second consider a supply shock. In case A, given a supply shock, fiscal policy can reduce the loss to a certain extent. In case B, given a supply shock, fiscal policy is ineffective.

Table 2.4
Fiscal Policy in Europe
A Supply Shock

Unemployment	0	Inflation	0
Structural Deficit	0		
Shock in A	6	Shock in B	6
Unemployment	6	Inflation	6
Structural Deficit	0		
Change in Govt Purchases	0		
Unemployment	6	Inflation	6
Structural Deficit	0		

Chapter 3
Interaction between Central Bank and Government A

1. The Model

An increase in European money supply lowers unemployment in Europe. On the other hand, it raises inflation there. However, it has no effect on the structural deficit. Correspondingly, an increase in European government purchases lowers unemployment in Europe. On the other hand, it raises inflation there. And what is more, it raises the structural deficit. The primary target of the European central bank is zero inflation in Europe. By contrast, the primary targets of the European government are zero unemployment and a zero structural deficit there.

The model of unemployment, inflation, and the structural deficit can be represented by a system of three equations:

$$u = A - M - G \tag{1}$$

$$\pi = B + M + G \tag{2}$$

$$s = G - T \tag{3}$$

Here u denotes the rate of unemployment in Europe, π is the rate of inflation in Europe, s is the structural deficit ratio in Europe, M is European money supply, G is European government purchases, T is European tax revenue at full-employment output, $G - T$ is the structural deficit in Europe, A is some other factors bearing on the rate of unemployment in Europe, and B is some other factors bearing on the rate of inflation in Europe. The endogenous variables are the rate of unemployment, the rate of inflation, and the structural deficit ratio.

According to equation (1), the rate of unemployment in Europe is a positive function of A, a negative function of European money supply, and a negative function of European government purchases. According to equation (2), the rate of inflation in Europe is a positive function of B, a positive function of European money supply, and a positive function of European government purchases. According to equation (3), the structural deficit ratio is a positive function of European government purchases. A unit increase in money supply lowers the rate of unemployment by 1 percentage point. On the other hand, it raises the rate of inflation by 1 percentage point. However, it has no effect on the structural deficit ratio. A unit increase in government purchases lowers the rate of unemployment by 1 percentage point. On the other hand, it raises the rate of inflation by 1 percentage point. And what is more, it raises the structural deficit ratio by 1 percentage point.

As to policy targets there are three distinct cases. In case A the target of the central bank is zero inflation. And the targets of the government are zero unemployment and a zero structural deficit. In case B the targets of the central bank are zero inflation and zero unemployment. And the targets of the government still are zero unemployment and a zero structural deficit. In case C the targets of the central bank are zero inflation and zero unemployment. And the targets of the government are zero unemployment, zero inflation, and a zero structural deficit. This chapter deals with case A, and the next chapters deal with cases B and C.

The target of the European central bank is zero inflation in Europe. The instrument of the European central bank is European money supply. By equation (2), the reaction function of the European central bank is:

$$M = -B - G \tag{4}$$

Suppose the European government raises European government purchases. Then, as a response, the European central bank lowers European money supply.

The targets of the European government are zero unemployment and a zero structural deficit in Europe. The instrument of the European government is European government purchases. There are two targets but only one instrument, so what is needed is a loss function. We assume that the European government has a quadratic loss function:

$$L_2 = u^2 + s^2 \tag{5}$$

L_2 is the loss to the European government caused by unemployment and the structural deficit. We assume equal weights in the loss function. The specific target of the European government is to minimize the loss, given the unemployment function and the structural deficit function. Taking account of equations (1) and (3), the loss function of the European government can be written as follows:

$$L_2 = (A - M - G)^2 + (G - T)^2 \tag{6}$$

Then the first-order condition for a minimum loss gives the reaction function of the European government:

$$2G = A + T - M \tag{7}$$

Suppose the European central bank lowers European money supply. Then, as a response, the European government raises European government purchases.

The Nash equilibrium is determined by the reaction functions of the European central bank and the European government. The solution to this problem is as follows:

$$M = -A - 2B - T \tag{8}$$

$$G = A + B + T \tag{9}$$

Equations (8) and (9) show the Nash equilibrium of European money supply and European government purchases. As a result, there is a unique Nash equilibrium. According to equations (8) and (9), an increase in A causes a reduction in money supply and an increase in government purchases. And the same applies to an increase in B.

From equations (1), (8) and (9) follows the equilibrium rate of unemployment in Europe:

$$u = A + B \tag{10}$$

From equations (2), (8) and (9) follows the equilibrium rate of inflation in Europe:

$$\pi = 0 \tag{11}$$

And from equations (3) and (9) follows the equilibrium structural deficit ratio in Europe:

$$s = A + B \tag{12}$$

Inflation in Europe is zero. By contrast, unemployment in Europe is not zero, nor is the structural deficit there.

2. Some Numerical Examples

For easy reference, the basic model is summarized here:

$$u = A - M - G \tag{1}$$
$$\pi = B + M + G \tag{2}$$
$$s = G - T \tag{3}$$

And the Nash equilibrium can be described by two equations:

$$M = -A - 2B - T \tag{4}$$
$$G = A + B + T \tag{5}$$

It proves useful to study two distinct cases:
- a demand shock in Europe
- a supply shock in Europe.

1) A demand shock in Europe. Let initial unemployment be zero, let initial inflation be zero, and let the initial structural deficit be zero as well. Step one refers to a decline in aggregate demand. In terms of the model there is an increase in A of 2 units and a decline in B of equally 2 units. Step two refers to the outside lag. Unemployment goes from zero to 2 percent. Inflation goes from zero to -2 percent. And the structural deficit stays at zero percent. Step three refers to the policy response. According to the Nash equilibrium there is an increase in money supply of 2 units and an increase in government purchases of zero units. Step four refers to the outside lag. Unemployment goes from 2 to zero percent. Inflation goes from -2 to zero percent. And the structural deficit stays at zero percent. Table 2.5 presents a synopsis.

As a result, given a demand shock, monetary and fiscal interaction can achieve zero inflation, zero unemployment, and a zero structural deficit. The loss functions of the central bank and the government are respectively:

$$L_1 = \pi^2 \tag{6}$$
$$L_2 = u^2 + s^2 \tag{7}$$

The initial loss of the central bank is zero, as is the initial loss of the government. The demand shock causes a loss to the central bank of 4 units and a loss to the government of equally 4 units. Then policy interaction can reduce the loss of the central bank and the government to zero each.

2) A supply shock in Europe. Let initial unemployment be zero, let initial inflation be zero, and let the initial structural deficit be zero as well. Step one refers to the supply shock. In terms of the model there is an increase in B of 2 units and an increase in A of equally 2 units. Step two refers to the outside lag. Inflation goes from zero to 2 percent. Unemployment goes from zero to 2 percent as well. And the structural deficit stays at zero percent. Step three refers to the policy response. According to the Nash equilibrium there is a reduction in money supply of 6 units and an increase in government purchases of 4 units. Step four refers to the outside lag. Inflation goes from 2 to zero percent. Unemployment goes from 2 to 4 percent. And the structural deficit goes from zero to 4 percent. Table 2.6 gives an overview.

Table 2.5
Interaction between Central Bank and Government
A Demand Shock

Unemployment	0	Inflation	0
Structural Deficit	0		
Shock in A	2	Shock in B	−2
Unemployment	2	Inflation	−2
Structural Deficit	0		
Change in Money Supply	2	Change in Govt Purchases	0
Unemployment	0	Inflation	0
Structural Deficit	0		

Table 2.6
Interaction between Central Bank and Government
A Supply Shock

Unemployment	0	Inflation	0
Structural Deficit	0		
Shock in A	2	Shock in B	2
Unemployment	2	Inflation	2
Structural Deficit	0		
Change in Money Supply	−6	Change in Govt Purchases	4
Unemployment	4	Inflation	0
Structural Deficit	4		

As a result, given a supply shock, monetary and fiscal interaction can achieve zero inflation. On the other hand, it causes an increase in unemployment and an increase in the structural deficit. The supply shock causes a loss to the central bank of 4 units and a loss to the government of equally 4 units. Then policy interaction reduces the loss of the central bank from 4 to zero units. However, it increases the loss of the government from 4 to 32 units. To sum up, policy interaction increases the total loss from 8 to 32 units.

3) Summary. Given a demand shock, policy interaction can achieve zero inflation, zero unemployment, and a zero structural deficit. Given a supply shock, policy interaction can achieve zero inflation. On the other hand, it causes an increase in both unemployment and the structural deficit.

Chapter 4
Interaction between Central Bank and Government B

1. The Model

This chapter deals with case B. The targets of the European central bank are zero inflation and zero unemployment. The targets of the European government are zero unemployment and a zero structural deficit. The model of unemployment, inflation, and the structural deficit can be characterized by a system of three equations:

$$u = A - M - G \tag{1}$$

$$\pi = B + M + G \tag{2}$$

$$s = G - T \tag{3}$$

The targets of the European central bank are zero inflation and zero unemployment in Europe. The instrument of the European central bank is European money supply. There are two targets but only one instrument, so what is needed is a loss function. We assume that the European central bank has a quadratic loss function:

$$L_1 = \pi^2 + u^2 \tag{4}$$

L_1 is the loss to the European central bank caused by inflation and unemployment. We assume equal weights in the loss function. The specific target of the European central bank is to minimize the loss, given the inflation function and the unemployment function. Taking account of equations (1) and (2), the loss function of the European central bank can be written as follows:

$$L_1 = (B + M + G)^2 + (A - M - G)^2 \tag{5}$$

Then the first-order condition for a minimum loss gives the reaction function of the European central bank:

$$2M = A - B - 2G \tag{6}$$

Suppose the European government raises European government purchases. Then, as a response, the European central bank lowers European money supply.

The targets of the European government are zero unemployment and a zero structural deficit in Europe. The instrument of the European government is European government purchases. There are two targets but only one instrument, so what is needed is a loss function. We assume that the European government has a quadratic loss function:

$$L_2 = u^2 + s^2 \tag{7}$$

L_2 is the loss to the European government caused by unemployment and the structural deficit. We assume equal weights in the loss function. The specific target of the European government is to minimize the loss, given the unemployment function and the structural deficit function. Taking account of equations (1) and (3), the loss function of the European government can be written as follows:

$$L_2 = (A - M - G)^2 + (G - T)^2 \tag{8}$$

Then the first-order condition for a minimum loss gives the reaction function of the European government:

$$2G = A + T - M \tag{9}$$

Suppose the European central bank lowers European money supply. Then, as a response, the European government raises European government purchases.

The Nash equilibrium is determined by the reaction functions of the European central bank and the European government. The solution to this problem is as follows:

$$M = -B - T \tag{10}$$

$$2G = A + B + 2T \tag{11}$$

Equations (10) and (11) show the Nash equilibrium of European money supply and European government purchases. As a result, there is a unique Nash equilibrium. According to equations (10) and (11), an increase in A causes an increase in government purchases. And an increase in B causes a reduction in money supply and an increase in government purchases.

From equations (1), (10) and (11) follows the equilibrium rate of unemployment in Europe:

$$2u = A + B \tag{12}$$

From equations (2), (10) and (11) follows the equilibrium rate of inflation in Europe:

$$2\pi = A + B \tag{13}$$

And from equations (3) and (11) follows the equilibrium structural deficit ratio in Europe:

$$2s = A + B \tag{14}$$

Unemployment in Europe is not zero. Inflation in Europe and the structural deficit there are not zero either.

2. Some Numerical Examples

For easy reference, the basic model is reproduced here:

$$u = A - M - G \tag{1}$$

$$\pi = B + M + G \tag{2}$$

$$s = G - T \tag{3}$$

And the Nash equilibrium can be described by two equations:

$$M = - B - T \tag{4}$$

$$2G = A + B + 2T \tag{5}$$

It proves useful to study two distinct cases:
- a demand shock in Europe
- a supply shock in Europe.

1) A demand shock in Europe. Let initial unemployment be zero, let initial inflation be zero, and let the initial structural deficit be zero as well. Step one refers to a decline in aggregate demand. In terms of the model there is an increase in A of 2 units and a decline in B of equally 2 units. Step two refers to the outside lag. Unemployment goes from zero to 2 percent. Inflation goes from zero to − 2 percent. And the structural deficit stays at zero percent. Step three refers to the policy response. According to the Nash equilibrium there is an increase in money supply of 2 units and an increase in government purchases of zero units. Step four refers to the outside lag. Unemployment goes from 2 to zero percent. Inflation goes from − 2 to zero percent. And the structural deficit stays at zero percent. Table 2.7 presents a synopsis.

As a result, given a demand shock, monetary and fiscal interaction can achieve zero inflation, zero unemployment, and a zero structural deficit. The loss functions of the central bank and the government are respectively:

$$L_1 = \pi^2 + u^2 \quad (6)$$
$$L_2 = u^2 + s^2 \quad (7)$$

The initial loss of the central bank is zero, as is the initial loss of the government. The demand shock causes a loss to the central bank of 8 units and a loss to the government of 4 units. Then policy interaction can reduce the loss of the central bank and the government to zero each.

Table 2.7
Interaction between Central Bank and Government
A Demand Shock

Unemployment	0	Inflation	0
Structural Deficit	0		
Shock in A	2	Shock in B	− 2
Unemployment	2	Inflation	− 2
Structural Deficit	0		
Change in Money Supply	2	Change in Govt Purchases	0
Unemployment	0	Inflation	0
Structural Deficit	0		

2) A supply shock in Europe. Let initial unemployment be zero, let initial inflation be zero, and let the initial structural deficit be zero as well. Step one refers to the supply shock. In terms of the model there is an increase in B of 2 units and an increase in A of equally 2 units. Step two refers to the outside lag. Inflation goes from zero to 2 percent. Unemployment goes from zero to 2 percent as well. And the structural deficit stays at zero percent. Step three refers to the policy response. According to the Nash equilibrium there is a reduction in money supply of 2 units and an increase in government purchases of equally 2 units. Step four refers to the outside lag. Inflation stays at 2 percent. Unemployment

stays at 2 percent as well. And the structural deficit goes from zero to 2 percent. Table 2.8 gives an overview.

As a result, given a supply shock, monetary and fiscal interaction has no effect on inflation and unemployment. And what is more, it causes an increase in the structural deficit. The supply shock causes a loss to the central bank of 8 units and a loss to the government of 4 units. However, policy interaction does not reduce the loss of the central bank. And what is more, it increases the loss of the government to 8 units. To sum up, policy interaction increases the total loss from 12 to 16 units.

Table 2.8
Interaction between Central Bank and Government
A Supply Shock

Unemployment	0	Inflation	0
Structural Deficit	0		
Shock in A	2	Shock in B	2
Unemployment	2	Inflation	2
Structural Deficit	0		
Change in Money Supply	−2	Change in Govt Purchases	2
Unemployment	2	Inflation	2
Structural Deficit	2		

3) Summary. Given a demand shock, policy interaction can achieve zero inflation, zero unemployment, and a zero structural deficit. Given a supply shock, policy interaction has no effect on inflation and unemployment. And what is more, it causes an increase in the structural deficit.

Chapter 5
Interaction between Central Bank and Government C

1. The Model

This chapter deals with case C. The targets of the European central bank are zero inflation and zero unemployment. The targets of the European government are zero unemployment, zero inflation, and a zero structural deficit. The model of unemployment, inflation, and the structural deficit can be represented by a system of three equations:

$$u = A - M - G \tag{1}$$

$$\pi = B + M + G \tag{2}$$

$$s = G - T \tag{3}$$

The targets of the European central bank are zero inflation and zero unemployment in Europe. The instrument of the European central bank is European money supply. There are two targets but only one instrument, so what is needed is a loss function. We assume that the European central bank has a quadratic loss function:

$$L_1 = \pi^2 + u^2 \tag{4}$$

L_1 is the loss to the European central bank caused by inflation and unemployment. We assume equal weights in the loss function. The specific target of the European central bank is to minimize the loss, given the inflation function and the unemployment function. Taking account of equations (1) and (2), the loss function of the European central bank can be written as follows:

$$L_1 = (B + M + G)^2 + (A - M - G)^2 \tag{5}$$

M. Carlberg et al., *Strategic Policy Interactions in a Monetary Union*,
DOI: 10.1007/978-3-540-92751-8_13, © Springer-Verlag Berlin Heidelberg 2009

Then the first-order condition for a minimum loss gives the reaction function of the European central bank:

$$2M = A - B - 2G \tag{6}$$

Suppose the European government raises European government purchases. Then, as a response, the European central bank lowers European money supply.

The targets of the European government are zero unemployment, zero inflation, and a zero structural deficit in Europe. The instrument of the European government is European government purchases. There are three targets but only one instrument, so what is needed is a loss function. We assume that the European government has a quadratic loss function:

$$L_2 = \pi^2 + u^2 + s^2 \tag{7}$$

L_2 is the loss to the European government caused by inflation, unemployment, and the structural deficit. We assume equal weights in the loss function. The specific target of the European government is to minimize the loss, given the inflation function, the unemployment function, and the structural deficit function. Taking account of equations (1), (2) and (3), the loss function of the European government can be written as follows:

$$L_2 = (B + M + G)^2 + (A - M - G)^2 + (G - T)^2 \tag{8}$$

Then the first-order condition for a minimum loss gives the reaction function of the European government:

$$3G = A + T - B - 2M \tag{9}$$

Suppose the European central bank lowers European money supply. Then, as a response, the European government raises European government purchases.

The Nash equilibrium is determined by the reaction functions of the European central bank and the European government. The solution to this problem is as follows:

$$2M = A - B - 2T \qquad (10)$$

$$G = T \qquad (11)$$

Equations (10) and (11) show the Nash equilibrium of European money supply and European government purchases. As a result, there is a unique Nash equilibrium. According to equations (10) and (11), an increase in A causes an increase in money supply. And an increase in B causes a reduction in money supply.

From equations (1), (10) and (11) follows the equilibrium rate of unemployment in Europe:

$$2u = A + B \qquad (12)$$

From equations (2), (10) and (11) follows the equilibrium rate of inflation in Europe:

$$2\pi = A + B \qquad (13)$$

And from equations (3) and (11) follows the equilibrium structural deficit ratio in Europe:

$$s = 0 \qquad (14)$$

The structural deficit in Europe is zero. By contrast, unemployment and inflation there are not zero.

2. Some Numerical Examples

For easy reference, the basic model is summarized here:

$$u = A - M - G \tag{1}$$

$$\pi = B + M + G \tag{2}$$

$$s = G - T \tag{3}$$

And the Nash equilibrium can be described by two equations:

$$2M = A - B - 2T \tag{4}$$

$$G = T \tag{5}$$

It proves useful to study two distinct cases:
- a demand shock in Europe
- a supply shock in Europe.

1) A demand shock in Europe. Let initial unemployment be zero, let initial inflation be zero, and let the initial structural deficit be zero as well. Step one refers to a decline in aggregate demand. In terms of the model there is an increase in A of 2 units and a decline in B of equally 2 units. Step two refers to the outside lag. Unemployment goes from zero to 2 percent. Inflation goes from zero to -2 percent. And the structural deficit stays at zero percent. Step three refers to the policy response. According to the Nash equilibrium there is an increase in money supply of 2 units and an increase in government purchases of zero units. Step four refers to the outside lag. Unemployment goes from 2 to zero percent. Inflation goes from -2 to zero percent. And the structural deficit stays at zero percent. Table 2.9 presents a synopsis.

As a result, given a demand shock, monetary and fiscal interaction can achieve zero inflation, zero unemployment, and a zero structural deficit. The loss functions of the central bank and the government are respectively:

$$L_1 = \pi^2 + u^2 \tag{6}$$

$$L_2 = \pi^2 + u^2 + s^2 \tag{7}$$

The initial loss of the central bank is zero, as is the initial loss of the government. The demand shock causes a loss to the central bank of 8 units and a loss to the government of equally 8 units. Then policy interaction can reduce the loss of the central bank and the government to zero each.

Table 2.9
Interaction between Central Bank and Government
A Demand Shock

Unemployment	0	Inflation	0
Structural Deficit	0		
Shock in A	2	Shock in B	− 2
Unemployment	2	Inflation	− 2
Structural Deficit	0		
Change in Money Supply	2	Change in Govt Purchases	0
Unemployment	0	Inflation	0
Structural Deficit	0		

2) A supply shock in Europe. Let initial unemployment be zero, let initial inflation be zero, and let the initial structural deficit be zero as well. Step one refers to the supply shock. In terms of the model there is an increase in B of 2 units and an increase in A of equally 2 units. Step two refers to the outside lag. Inflation goes from zero to 2 percent. Unemployment goes from zero to 2 percent as well. And the structural deficit stays at zero percent. Step three refers to the policy response. According to the Nash equilibrium there is no change in money supply and no change in government purchases. Step four refers to the outside

lag. Inflation stays at 2 percent. Unemployment stays at 2 percent as well. And the structural deficit stays at zero percent. Table 2.10 gives an overview.

As a result, given a supply shock, monetary and fiscal interaction is ineffective. The supply shock causes a loss to the central bank of 8 units and a loss to the government of equally 8 units. However, policy interaction cannot reduce the loss to the central bank and the government.

Table 2.10
Interaction between Central Bank and Government
A Supply Shock

Unemployment	0	Inflation	0
Structural Deficit	0		
Shock in A	2	Shock in B	2
Unemployment	2	Inflation	2
Structural Deficit	0		
Change in Money Supply	0	Change in Govt Purchases	0
Unemployment	2	Inflation	2
Structural Deficit	0		

3) Summary. Given a demand shock, policy interaction can achieve zero inflation, zero unemployment, and a zero structural deficit. Given a supply shock, policy interaction is ineffective.

4) Comparing cases A, B and C. As to the policy targets there are three distinct cases. In case A the target of the central bank is zero inflation. And the targets of the government are zero unemployment and a zero structural deficit. In case B the targets of the central bank are zero inflation and zero unemployment. And the targets of the government still are zero unemployment and a zero structural deficit. In case C the targets of the central bank are zero inflation and

zero unemployment. And the targets of the government are zero unemployment, zero inflation, and a zero structural deficit.

First consider a demand shock. In case A, given a demand shock, policy interaction can achieve zero inflation, zero unemployment, and a zero structural deficit. In case B, given a demand shock, policy interaction has the same effects as in case A. And the same holds for case C. Second consider a supply shock. In case A, given a supply shock, policy interaction can achieve zero inflation. On the other hand, it causes an increase in both unemployment and the structural deficit. In case B, given a supply shock, policy interaction has no effect on inflation and unemployment. And what is more, it causes an increase in the structural deficit. In case C, given a supply shock, policy interaction is ineffective.

Chapter 6
Cooperation between Central Bank and Government

1. The Model

The model of unemployment, inflation, and the structural deficit can be characterized by a system of three equations:

$$u = A - M - G \tag{1}$$

$$\pi = B + M + G \tag{2}$$

$$s = G - T \tag{3}$$

The policy makers are the European central bank and the European government. The targets of policy cooperation are zero inflation, zero unemployment, and a zero structural deficit. The instruments of policy cooperation are European money supply and European government purchases. There are three targets but only two instruments, so what is needed is a loss function:

$$L = \pi^2 + u^2 + s^2 \tag{4}$$

L is the loss caused by inflation, unemployment, and the structural deficit. We assume equal weights in the loss function. The specific target of policy cooperation is to minimize the loss, given the inflation function, the unemployment function, and the structural deficit function. Taking account of equations (1), (2) and (3), the loss function under policy cooperation can be written as follows:

$$L = (B + M + G)^2 + (A - M - G)^2 + (G - T)^2 \tag{5}$$

Then the first-order conditions for a minimum loss are:

$$2M = A - B - 2G \qquad (6)$$

$$3G = A + T - B - 2M \qquad (7)$$

Equation (6) shows the first-order condition with respect to European money supply. And equation (7) shows the first-order condition with respect to European government purchases.

The cooperative equilibrium is determined by the first-order conditions for a minimum loss. The solution to this problem is as follows:

$$2M = A - B - 2T \qquad (8)$$

$$G = T \qquad (9)$$

Equations (8) and (9) show the cooperative equilibrium of European money supply and European government purchases. As a result, there is a unique cooperative equilibrium. An increase in A causes an increase in money supply. And an increase in B causes a reduction in money supply.

From equations (1), (8) and (9) follows the optimum rate of unemployment in Europe:

$$2u = A + B \qquad (10)$$

From equations (2), (8) and (9) follows the optimum rate of inflation in Europe:

$$2\pi = A + B \qquad (11)$$

And from equations (3) and (9) follows the optimum structural deficit ratio in Europe:

$$s = 0 \qquad (12)$$

The structural deficit in Europe is zero. By contrast, unemployment and inflation there are not zero.

2. Some Numerical Examples

For easy reference, the basic model is reproduced here:

$$u = A - M - G \tag{1}$$

$$\pi = B + M + G \tag{2}$$

$$s = G - T \tag{3}$$

And the cooperative equilibrium can be described by two equations:

$$2M = A - B - 2T \tag{4}$$

$$G = T \tag{5}$$

It proves useful to study two distinct cases:
- a demand shock in Europe
- a supply shock in Europe.

1) A demand shock in Europe. Let initial unemployment be zero, let initial inflation be zero, and let the initial structural deficit be zero as well. Step one refers to a decline in aggregate demand. In terms of the model there is an increase in A of 2 units and a decline in B of equally 2 units. Step two refers to the outside lag. Unemployment goes from zero to 2 percent. Inflation goes from zero to − 2 percent. And the structural deficit stays at zero percent. Step three refers to the policy response. What is needed, according to the model, is an increase in money supply of 2 units and an increase in government purchases of zero units. Step four refers to the outside lag. Unemployment goes from 2 to zero percent. Inflation goes from − 2 to zero percent. And the structural deficit stays at zero percent. For a synopsis see Table 2.11.

As a result, given a demand shock, monetary and fiscal cooperation can achieve zero inflation, zero unemployment, and a zero structural deficit. The loss function under policy cooperation is:

$$L = \pi^2 + u^2 + s^2 \tag{6}$$

The initial loss is zero. The demand shock causes a loss of 8 units. Then policy cooperation can reduce the loss to zero.

2) A supply shock in Europe. Let initial unemployment be zero, let initial inflation be zero, and let the initial structural deficit be zero as well. Step one refers to the supply shock. In terms of the model there is an increase in B of 2 units and an increase in A of equally 2 units. Step two refers to the outside lag. Inflation goes from zero to 2 percent. Unemployment goes from zero to 2 percent as well. And the structural deficit stays at zero percent. Step three refers to the policy response. What is needed, according to the model, is to hold money supply and government purchases constant. Step four refers to the outside lag. Inflation stays at 2 percent. Unemployment stays a 2 percent as well. And the structural deficit stays at zero percent. For an overview see Table 2.12.

As a result, given a supply shock, monetary and fiscal cooperation is ineffective. The supply shock causes a loss of 8 units. However, policy cooperation cannot reduce the loss.

3) Summary. Given a demand shock, policy cooperation can achieve zero inflation, zero unemployment, and a zero structural deficit. Given a supply shock, policy cooperation is ineffective.

4) Comparing policy cooperation with policy interaction. First consider the targets of policy interaction. By assumption, the target of the central bank is zero inflation. And the targets of the government are zero unemployment and a zero structural deficit. There are equal weights in the loss function of the government. Second consider the targets of policy cooperation. By assumption, the targets are zero inflation, zero unemployment, and a zero structural deficit. There are equal weights in the common loss function.

Now consider a demand shock. Given a demand shock, policy interaction can achieve zero inflation, zero unemployment, and a zero structural deficit. Given a demand shock, policy cooperation has the same effects as policy interaction. Then consider a supply shock. Given a supply shock, policy interaction can achieve zero inflation. On the other hand, it causes an increase in both unemployment and the structural deficit. By contrast, given a supply shock, policy cooperation is ineffective.

Table 2.11
Cooperation between Central Bank and Government
A Demand Shock

Unemployment	0	Inflation	0
Structural Deficit	0		
Shock in A	2	Shock in B	− 2
Unemployment	2	Inflation	− 2
Structural Deficit	0		
Change in Money Supply	2	Change in Govt Purchases	0
Unemployment	0	Inflation	0
Structural Deficit	0		

Table 2.12
Cooperation between Central Bank and Government
A Supply Shock

Unemployment	0	Inflation	0
Structural Deficit	0		
Shock in A	2	Shock in B	2
Unemployment	2	Inflation	2
Structural Deficit	0		
Change in Money Supply	0	Change in Govt Purchases	0
Unemployment	2	Inflation	2
Structural Deficit	0		

Part Three

The Monetary Union of Two Countries

Absence of a Deficit Target

Chapter 1
Monetary Policy in Europe A

1. The Model

For ease of exposition we assume that the monetary union consists of two countries, say Germany and France. The member countries are the same size and have the same behavioural functions. An increase in European money supply lowers unemployment in Germany and France. On the other hand, it raises producer inflation there. Here producer inflation in Germany refers to the price of German goods. Similarly, producer inflation in France refers to the price of French goods.

The model of unemployment and inflation can be represented by a system of four equations:

$$u_1 = A_1 - M \tag{1}$$

$$u_2 = A_2 - M \tag{2}$$

$$\pi_1 = B_1 + M \tag{3}$$

$$\pi_2 = B_2 + M \tag{4}$$

Of course this is a reduced form. Here u_1 denotes the rate of unemployment in Germany, u_2 is the rate of unemployment in France, π_1 is the rate of inflation in Germany, π_2 is the rate of inflation in France, M is European money supply, A_1 is some other factors bearing on the rate of unemployment in Germany, A_2 is some other factors bearing on the rate of unemployment in France, B_1 is some other factors bearing on the rate of inflation in Germany, and B_2 is some other factors bearing on the rate of inflation in France. The endogenous variables are the rate of unemployment in Germany, the rate of unemployment in France, the rate of inflation in Germany, and the rate of inflation in France.

According to equation (1), the rate of unemployment in Germany is a positive function of A_1 and a negative function of European money supply.

98

According to equation (2), the rate of unemployment in France is a positive function of A_2 and a negative function of European money supply. According to equation (3), the rate of inflation in Germany is a positive function of B_1 and a positive function of European money supply. According to equation (4), the rate of inflation in France is a positive function of B_2 and a positive function of European money supply.

A unit increase in European money supply lowers the rates of unemployment in Germany and France by 1 percentage point each. On the other hand, it raises the rates of inflation there by 1 percentage point each. For instance, let initial unemployment in Germany be 3 percent, and let initial unemployment in France be 1 percent. Further let initial inflation in Germany be 3 percent, and let initial inflation in France be 1 percent. Now consider a unit increase in European money supply. Then unemployment in Germany goes from 3 to 2 percent, and unemployment in France goes from 1 to zero percent. On the other hand, inflation in Germany goes from 3 to 4 percent, and inflation in France goes from 1 to 2 percent.

As to policy targets there are two distinct cases. In case A the targets of the European central bank are zero inflation in each of the member countries. In case B the targets of the European central bank are zero inflation and zero unemployment in each of the member countries. This chapter deals with case A, and the next chapter deals with case B.

The targets of the European central bank are zero inflation in Germany and France respectively. The instrument of the European central bank is European money supply. There are two targets but only one instrument, so what is needed is a loss function. We assume that the European central bank has a quadratic loss function:

$$L = \pi_1^2 + \pi_2^2 \tag{5}$$

L is the loss to the European central bank caused by inflation in Germany and France. We assume equal weights in the loss function. The specific target of the European central bank is to minimize the loss, given the inflation functions. Taking account of equations (3) and (4), the loss function of the European central bank can be written as follows:

$$L = (B_1 + M)^2 + (B_2 + M)^2 \tag{6}$$

Then the first-order condition for a minimum loss is:

$$2M = -B_1 - B_2 \tag{7}$$

Here M is the optimum level of European money supply. An increase in A_1 requires no change in European money supply. And an increase in B_1 requires a cut in European money supply.

From equations (1) and (7) follows the optimum rate of unemployment in Germany:

$$2u_1 = 2A_1 + B_1 + B_2 \tag{8}$$

And from equations (2) and (7) follows the optimum rate of unemployment in France:

$$2u_2 = 2A_2 + B_1 + B_2 \tag{9}$$

By definition, the rate of unemployment in Europe is:

$$u = 0.5u_1 + 0.5u_2 \tag{10}$$

Making use of equations (8) and (9), the optimum rate of unemployment in Europe is:

$$2u = A_1 + A_2 + B_1 + B_2 \tag{11}$$

From equations (3) and (7) follows the optimum rate of inflation in Germany:

$$2\pi_1 = B_1 - B_2 \tag{12}$$

And from equations (4) and (7) follows the optimum rate of inflation in France:

$$2\pi_2 = B_2 - B_1 \tag{13}$$

By definition, the rate of inflation in Europe is:

$$\pi = 0.5\pi_1 + 0.5\pi_2 \tag{14}$$

Making use of equations (12) and (13), the optimum rate of inflation in Europe is:

$$\pi = 0 \tag{15}$$

Inflation in Europe is zero. However, inflation in Germany and France is not zero. And what is more, unemployment in Germany, France and Europe is not zero either.

2. Some Numerical Examples

For easy reference, the model of unemployment and inflation is summarized here:

$$u_1 = A_1 - M \tag{1}$$

$$u_2 = A_2 - M \tag{2}$$

$$\pi_1 = B_1 + M \tag{3}$$

$$\pi_2 = B_2 + M \tag{4}$$

And the optimum level of European money supply is:

$$2M = -B_1 - B_2 \tag{5}$$

It proves useful to study three distinct cases:
- a demand shock in Germany
- a supply shock in Germany
- a common demand shock in Europe.

1) A demand shock in Germany. In each of the member countries, let initial unemployment be zero, and let initial inflation be zero as well. Step one refers to a decline in the demand for German goods. In terms of the model there is an increase in A_1 of 2 units and a decline in B_1 of equally 2 units. Step two refers to the outside lag. Unemployment in Germany goes from zero to 2 percent. Unemployment in France stays at zero percent. Inflation in Germany goes from zero to − 2 percent. And inflation in France stays at zero percent.

Step three refers to the policy response. What is needed, according to the model, is an increase in European money supply of 1 unit. Step four refers to the outside lag. Unemployment in Germany goes from 2 to 1 percent. Unemployment in France goes from zero to − 1 percent. Thus unemployment in Europe goes from 1 to zero percent. Inflation in Germany goes from − 2 to − 1 percent. Inflation in France goes from zero to 1 percent. Thus inflation in Europe goes from − 1 to zero percent. Table 3.1 presents a synopsis.

Table 3.1
Monetary Policy in Europe
A Demand Shock in Germany

Germany		France	
Unemployment	0	Unemployment	0
Inflation	0	Inflation	0
Shock in A$_1$	2		
Shock in B$_1$	− 2		
Unemployment	2	Unemployment	0
Inflation	− 2	Inflation	0
Δ European Money Supply	1		
Unemployment	1	Unemployment	− 1
Inflation	− 1	Inflation	1

As a result, given a demand shock in Germany, monetary policy in Europe can achieve zero inflation in Europe as a whole. However, it cannot achieve zero inflation in Germany and France. The loss function of the European central bank is:

$$L = \pi_1^2 + \pi_2^2 \tag{6}$$

The initial loss is zero. The demand shock in Germany causes a loss of 4 units. Then monetary policy in Europe can reduce the loss to 2 units.

2) A supply shock in Germany. In each of the member countries, let initial unemployment be zero, and let initial inflation be zero as well. Step one refers to

the supply shock in Germany. In terms of the model there is an increase in B_1 of 2 units and an increase in A_1 of equally 2 units. Step two refers to the outside lag. Inflation in Germany goes from zero to 2 percent. Inflation in France stays at zero percent. Unemployment in Germany goes from zero to 2 percent. And unemployment in France stays at zero percent.

Step three refers to the policy response. What is needed, according to the model, is a reduction in European money supply of 1 unit. Step four refers to the outside lag. Inflation in Germany goes from 2 to 1 percent. Inflation in France goes from zero to − 1 percent. So inflation in Europe goes from 1 to zero percent. Unemployment in Germany goes from 2 to 3 percent. Unemployment in France goes from zero to 1 percent. So unemployment in Europe goes from 1 to 2 percent. Table 3.2 gives an overview.

Table 3.2
Monetary Policy in Europe
A Supply Shock in Germany

Germany		France	
Unemployment	0	Unemployment	0
Inflation	0	Inflation	0
Shock in A_1	2		
Shock in B_1	2		
Unemployment	2	Unemployment	0
Inflation	2	Inflation	0
Δ European Money Supply	− 1		
Unemployment	3	Unemployment	1
Inflation	1	Inflation	− 1

As a result, given a supply shock in Germany, monetary policy in Europe can achieve zero inflation in Europe as a whole. However, it cannot achieve zero inflation in Germany and France. And what is more, it causes an increase in European unemployment. The supply shock in Germany causes a loss of 4 units. Then monetary policy in Europe can reduce the loss to 2 units.

3) A common demand shock in Europe. In each of the member countries, let initial unemployment be zero, and let initial inflation be zero as well. Step one refers to a decline in the common demand for European goods. In terms of the model there is an increase in A_1 of 2 units, an increase in A_2 of 2 units, a decline in B_1 of 2 units, and a decline in B_2 of equally 2 units. Step two refers to the outside lag. Unemployment in Germany goes from zero to 2 percent, as does unemployment in France. Inflation in Germany goes from zero to − 2 percent, as does inflation in France.

Step three refers to the policy response. What is needed, according to the model, is an increase in European money supply of 2 units. Step four refers to the outside lag. Unemployment in Germany goes from 2 to zero percent, as does unemployment in France. Inflation in Germany goes from − 2 to zero percent, as does inflation France. For a synopsis see Table 3.3. As a result, given a common demand shock in Europe, monetary policy in Europe can achieve zero inflation in Germany and France.

4) Summary. Given a demand shock in Germany, monetary policy in Europe can achieve zero inflation in Europe as a whole. However, it cannot achieve zero inflation in Germany and France. Given a supply shock in Germany, monetary policy in Europe can achieve zero inflation in Europe as a whole. However, it cannot achieve zero inflation in Germany and France. And what is more, it causes an increase in European unemployment. Given a common demand shock in Europe, monetary policy in Europe can achieve zero inflation in Germany and France.

Table 3.3

Monetary Policy in Europe

A Common Demand Shock in Europe

Germany		France	
Unemployment	0	Unemployment	0
Inflation	0	Inflation	0
Shock in A_1	2	Shock in A_2	2
Shock in B_1	-2	Shock in B_2	-2
Unemployment	2	Unemployment	2
Inflation	-2	Inflation	-2
Δ European Money Supply	2		
Unemployment	0	Unemployment	0
Inflation	0	Inflation	0

Chapter 2
Monetary Policy in Europe B

1. The Model

The model of unemployment and inflation can be characterized by a system of four equations:

$$u_1 = A_1 - M \tag{1}$$

$$u_2 = A_2 - M \tag{2}$$

$$\pi_1 = B_1 + M \tag{3}$$

$$\pi_2 = B_2 + M \tag{4}$$

The targets of the European central bank are zero inflation and zero unemployment in each of the member countries. The instrument of the European central bank is European money supply. There are four targets but only one instrument, so what is needed is a loss function. We assume that the European central bank has a quadratic loss function:

$$L = \pi_1^2 + \pi_2^2 + u_1^2 + u_2^2 \tag{5}$$

L is the loss to the European central bank caused by inflation and unemployment in each of the member countries. We assume equal weights in the loss function. The specific target of the European central bank is to minimize the loss, given the inflation functions and the unemployment functions. Taking account of equations (1), (2), (3) and (4), the loss function of the European central bank can be written as follows:

$$L = (B_1 + M)^2 + (B_2 + M)^2 + (A_1 - M)^2 + (A_2 - M)^2 \tag{6}$$

Then the first-order condition for a minimum loss is:

$$4M = A_1 + A_2 - B_1 - B_2 \tag{7}$$

Here M is the optimum level of European money supply. An increase in A_1 requires an increase in European money supply. And an increase in B_1 requires a cut in European money supply.

From equations (1) and (7) follows the optimum rate of unemployment in Germany:

$$4u_1 = 3A_1 - A_2 + B_1 + B_2 \tag{8}$$

And from equations (2) and (7) follows the optimum rate of unemployment in France:

$$4u_2 = -A_1 + 3A_2 + B_1 + B_2 \tag{9}$$

By definition, the rate of unemployment in Europe is:

$$u = 0.5u_1 + 0.5u_2 \tag{10}$$

Making use of equations (8) and (9), the optimum rate of unemployment in Europe is:

$$4u = A_1 + A_2 + B_1 + B_2 \tag{11}$$

From equations (3) and (7) follows the optimum rate of inflation in Germany:

$$4\pi_1 = A_1 + A_2 + 3B_1 - B_2 \tag{12}$$

And from equations (4) and (7) follows the optimum rate of inflation in France:

$$4\pi_2 = A_1 + A_2 - B_1 + 3B_2 \tag{13}$$

By definition, the rate of inflation in Europe is:

$$\pi = 0.5\pi_1 + 0.5\pi_2 \tag{14}$$

Making use of equations (12) and (13), the optimum rate of inflation in Europe is:

$$4\pi = A_1 + A_2 + B_1 + B_2 \tag{15}$$

Unemployment in Germany, France and Europe is not zero, nor is inflation there.

2. Some Numerical Examples

For easy reference, the model of unemployment and inflation is reproduced here:

$$u_1 = A_1 - M \tag{1}$$

$$u_2 = A_2 - M \tag{2}$$

$$\pi_1 = B_1 + M \tag{3}$$

$$\pi_2 = B_2 + M \tag{4}$$

And the optimum level of European money supply is:

$$4M = A_1 + A_2 - B_1 - B_2 \tag{5}$$

It proves useful to study three distinct cases:
- a demand shock in Germany
- a supply shock in Germany
- a common demand shock in Europe.

1) A demand shock in Germany. In each of the member countries, let initial unemployment be zero, and let initial inflation be zero as well. Step one refers to a decline in the demand for German goods. In terms of the model there is an increase in A_1 of 2 units and a decline in B_1 of equally 2 units. Step two refers to the outside lag. Unemployment in Germany goes from zero to 2 percent. Unemployment in France stays at zero percent. Inflation in Germany goes from zero to − 2 percent. And inflation in France stays a zero percent.

Step three refers to the policy response. What is needed, according to the model, is an increase in European money supply of 1 unit. Step four refers to the outside lag. Unemployment in Germany goes from 2 to 1 percent. Unemployment in France goes from zero to − 1 percent. Thus unemployment in Europe goes from 1 to zero percent. Inflation in Germany goes from − 2 to − 1 percent. Inflation in France goes from zero to 1 percent. Thus inflation in Europe goes from − 1 to zero percent. Table 3.4 presents a synopsis.

Table 3.4
Monetary Policy in Europe
A Demand Shock in Germany

Germany		France	
Unemployment	0	Unemployment	0
Inflation	0	Inflation	0
Shock in A_1	2		
Shock in B_1	− 2		
Unemployment	2	Unemployment	0
Inflation	− 2	Inflation	0
Δ European Money Supply	1		
Unemployment	1	Unemployment	− 1
Inflation	− 1	Inflation	1

As a result, given a demand shock in Germany, monetary policy in Europe can achieve zero inflation and zero unemployment in Europe as a whole. However, it cannot do so in each of the member countries. The loss function of the European central bank is:

$$L = \pi_1^2 + \pi_2^2 + u_1^2 + u_2^2 \tag{6}$$

The initial loss is zero. The demand shock in Germany causes a loss of 8 units. Then monetary policy in Europe can reduce the loss to 4 units.

2) A supply shock in Germany. In each of the member countries, let initial unemployment be zero, and let initial inflation be zero as well. Step one refers to

the supply shock in Germany. In terms of the model there is an increase in B_1 of 2 units and an increase in A_1 of equally 2 units. Step two refers to the outside lag. Inflation in Germany goes from zero to 2 percent. Inflation in France stays at zero percent. Unemployment in Germany goes from zero to 2 percent. And unemployment in France stays at zero percent.

Step three refers to the policy response. What is needed, according to the model, is to hold European money supply constant. Step four refers to the outside lag. Inflation in Germany stays at 2 percent, and inflation in France stays at zero percent. Thus inflation in Europe stays at 1 percent. Unemployment in Germany stays at 2 percent, and unemployment in France stays at zero percent. Thus unemployment in Europe stays at 1 percent. Table 3.5 gives an overview.

Table 3.5
Monetary Policy in Europe
A Supply Shock in Germany

Germany		France	
Unemployment	0	Unemployment	0
Inflation	0	Inflation	0
Shock in A_1	2		
Shock in B_1	2		
Unemployment	2	Unemployment	0
Inflation	2	Inflation	0
Δ European Money Supply	0		
Unemployment	2	Unemployment	0
Inflation	2	Inflation	0

As a result, given a supply shock in Germany, monetary policy in Europe is ineffective. The supply shock in Germany causes a loss of 8 units. However, monetary policy in Europe cannot reduce the loss.

3) A common demand shock in Europe. In each of the member countries, let initial unemployment be zero, and let initial inflation be zero as well. Step one refers to a decline in the common demand for European goods. In terms of the model there is an increase in A_1 of 2 units, an increase in A_2 of 2 units, a decline in B_1 of 2 units, and a decline in B_2 of equally 2 units. Step two refers to the outside lag. Unemployment in Germany goes from zero to 2 percent, as does unemployment in France. Inflation in Germany goes from zero to -2 percent, as does inflation in France.

Step three refers to the policy response. What is needed, according to the model, is an increase in European money supply of 2 units. Step four refers to the outside lag. Unemployment in Germany goes from 2 to zero percent, as does unemployment in France. Inflation in Germany goes from -2 to zero percent, as does inflation France. As a result, given a common demand shock in Europe, monetary policy in Europe can achieve zero inflation and zero unemployment in each of the member countries.

4) Summary. Given a demand shock in Germany, monetary policy in Europe can achieve zero inflation and zero unemployment in Europe as a whole. However, it cannot do so in each of the member countries. Given a supply shock in Germany, monetary policy in Europe is ineffective. Given a common demand shock in Europe, monetary policy in Europe can achieve zero inflation and zero unemployment in each of the member countries.

5) Comparing cases A and B. As to the policy targets there are two distinct cases. In case A, by definition, the targets of the European central bank are zero inflation in each of the member countries. In case B, by definition, the targets of the European central bank are zero inflation and zero unemployment in each of the member countries. First consider a demand shock in Germany. In case A, given a demand shock in Germany, monetary policy in Europe can achieve zero inflation and zero unemployment in Europe as a whole. However, it cannot do so in each of the member countries. In case B, given a demand shock in Germany, monetary policy in Europe has the same effects as in case A. Second consider a

supply shock in Germany. In case A, given a supply shock in Germany, monetary policy in Europe can achieve zero inflation in Europe as a whole. However, it cannot do so in each of the member countries. And what is more, it causes an increase in European unemployment. In case B, given a supply shock in Germany, monetary policy in Europe is ineffective.

Chapter 3
Fiscal Policy in Germany A

1. The Model

The monetary union consists of two countries, say Germany and France. The member countries are the same size and have the same behavioural functions. An increase in German government purchases lowers unemployment in Germany. On the other hand, it raises producer inflation there. For ease of exposition we assume that fiscal policy in one of the countries has no effect on unemployment or producer inflation in the other country.

The model of unemployment and inflation can be represented by a system of two equations:

$$u_1 = A_1 - G_1 \tag{1}$$
$$\pi_1 = B_1 + G_1 \tag{2}$$

Here u_1 denotes the rate of unemployment in Germany, π_1 is the rate of inflation in Germany, G_1 is German government purchases, A_1 is some other factors bearing on the rate of unemployment in Germany, and B_1 is some other factors bearing on the rate of inflation in Germany. The endogenous variables are the rate of unemployment and the rate of inflation in Germany.

According to equation (1), the rate of unemployment in Germany is a positive function of A_1 and a negative function of German government purchases. According to equation (2), the rate of inflation in Germany is a positive function of B_1 and a positive function of German government purchases.

A unit increase in government purchases lowers the rate of unemployment by 1 percentage point. On the other hand, it raises the rate of inflation by 1 percentage point. For instance, let initial unemployment be 2 percent, and let initial inflation be 2 percent as well. Now consider a unit increase in government purchases. Then unemployment goes from 2 to 1 percent. On the other hand, inflation goes from 2 to 3 percent.

As to policy targets there are two distinct cases. In case A the target of the government is zero unemployment. In case B the targets of the government are zero unemployment and zero inflation. This chapter deals with case A, and the next chapter deals with case B.

The target of the German government is zero unemployment in Germany. The instrument of the German government is German government purchases. By equation (1), the optimum level of German government purchases is:

$$G_1 = A_1 \tag{3}$$

That is, an increase in A_1 requires an increase in German government purchases. And an increase in B_1 requires no change in German government purchases. From equations (1) and (3) follows the optimum rate of unemployment in Germany:

$$u_1 = 0 \tag{4}$$

And from equations (2) and (3) follows the optimum rate of inflation in Germany:

$$\pi_1 = A_1 + B_1 \tag{5}$$

Unemployment in Germany is zero. By contrast, inflation there is not zero.

2. Some Numerical Examples

For easy reference, the model of unemployment and inflation is summarized here:

$$u_1 = A_1 - G_1 \tag{1}$$
$$\pi_1 = B_1 + G_1 \tag{2}$$

And the optimum level of German government purchases is:

$$G_1 = A_1 \tag{3}$$

It proves useful to study two distinct cases:
- a demand shock in Germany
- a supply shock in Germany.

1) A demand shock in Germany. Let initial unemployment in Germany be zero, and let initial inflation there be zero as well. Step one refers to a decline in the demand for German goods. In terms of the model there is an increase in A_1 of 1 unit and a decline in B_1 of equally 1 unit. Step two refers to the outside lag. Unemployment in Germany goes from zero to 1 percent. And inflation in Germany goes from zero to -1 percent. Step three refers to the policy response. What is needed, according to the model, is an increase in German government purchases of 1 unit. Step four refers to the outside lag. Unemployment in Germany goes from 1 to zero percent. And inflation in Germany goes from -1 to zero percent. Table 3.6 presents a synopsis.

As a result, given a demand shock in Germany, fiscal policy in Germany can achieve zero unemployment. And what is more, as a side effect, it can achieve zero inflation. The loss function of the German government is:

$$L_1 = u_1^2 \tag{4}$$

The initial loss is zero. The demand shock in Germany causes a loss of 1 unit. Then fiscal policy in Germany can reduce the loss to zero.

Table 3.6
Fiscal Policy in Germany
A Demand Shock

Unemployment	0	Inflation	0
Shock in A_1	1	Shock in B_1	-1
Unemployment	1	Inflation	-1
Change in Govt Purchases	1		
Unemployment	0	Inflation	0

2) A supply shock in Germany. Let initial unemployment and inflation in Germany be zero each. Step one refers to the supply shock in Germany. In terms of the model there is an increase in B_1 of 1 unit and an increase in A_1 of equally 1 unit. Step two refers to the outside lag. Inflation in Germany goes from zero to 1 percent. And unemployment there goes from zero to 1 percent as well. Step three refers to the policy response. What is needed, according to the model, is an increase in German government purchases of 1 unit. Step four refers to the outside lag. Unemployment in Germany goes from 1 to zero percent. And inflation in Germany goes from 1 to 2 percent. Table 3.7 gives an overview.

As a result, given a supply shock in Germany, fiscal policy in Germany can achieve zero unemployment. However, as a side effect, it causes an increase in inflation. The supply shock in Germany causes a loss of 1 unit. Then fiscal policy in Germany can reduce the loss to zero.

3) Summary. Given a demand shock in Germany, fiscal policy can achieve zero unemployment. And what is more, as a side effect, it can achieve zero inflation. Given a supply shock in Germany, fiscal policy can achieve zero unemployment. However, as a side effect, it causes an increase in inflation.

Table 3.7
Fiscal Policy in Germany
A Supply Shock

Unemployment	0	Inflation	0
Shock in A_1	1	Shock in B_1	1
Unemployment	1	Inflation	1
Change in Govt Purchases	1		
Unemployment	0	Inflation	2

Chapter 4
Fiscal Policy in Germany B

1. The Model

The model of unemployment and inflation can be characterized by a system of two equations:

$$u_1 = A_1 - G_1 \tag{1}$$
$$\pi_1 = B_1 + G_1 \tag{2}$$

The targets of the German government are zero unemployment and zero inflation in Germany. The instrument of the German government is German government purchases. There are two targets but only one instrument, so what is needed is a loss function. We assume that the German government has a quadratic loss function:

$$L_1 = \pi_1^2 + u_1^2 \tag{3}$$

L_1 is the loss to the German government caused by inflation and unemployment. We assume equal weights in the loss function. The specific target of the German government is to minimize the loss, given the inflation function and the unemployment function. Taking account of equations (1) and (2), the loss function of the German government can be written as follows:

$$L_1 = (B_1 + G_1)^2 + (A_1 - G_1)^2 \tag{4}$$

Then the first-order condition for a minimum loss is:

$$2G_1 = A_1 - B_1 \tag{5}$$

Here G_1 is the optimum level of German government purchases. An increase in A_1 requires an increase in German government purchases. And an increase in

B_1 requires a cut in German government purchases. From equations (1) and (5) follows the optimum rate of unemployment in Germany:

$$2u_1 = A_1 + B_1 \qquad (6)$$

And from equations (2) and (5) follows the optimum rate of inflation in Germany:

$$2\pi_1 = A_1 + B_1 \qquad (7)$$

Unemployment in Germany is not zero, nor is inflation there.

2. Some Numerical Examples

For easy reference, the model of unemployment and inflation is reproduced here:

$$u_1 = A_1 - G_1 \qquad (1)$$
$$\pi_1 = B_1 + G_1 \qquad (2)$$

And the optimum level of German government purchases is:

$$2G_1 = A_1 - B_1 \qquad (3)$$

It proves useful to study two distinct cases:
- a demand shock in Germany
- a supply shock in Germany.

1) A demand shock in Germany. Let initial unemployment in Germany be zero, and let initial inflation there be zero as well. Step one refers to a decline in the demand for German goods. In terms of the model there is an increase in A_1

of 1 unit and a decline in B_1 of equally 1 unit. Step two refers to the outside lag. Unemployment in Germany goes from zero to 1 percent. And inflation in Germany goes from zero to -1 percent. Step three refers to the policy response. What is needed, according to the model, is an increase in German government purchases of 1 unit. Step four refers to the outside lag. Unemployment in Germany goes from 1 to zero percent. And inflation in Germany goes from -1 to zero percent. Table 3.8 presents a synopsis.

As a result, given a demand shock in Germany, fiscal policy in Germany can achieve both zero unemployment and zero inflation. The loss function of the German government is:

$$L_1 = \pi_1^2 + u_1^2 \qquad (4)$$

The initial loss is zero. The demand shock in Germany causes a loss of 2 units. Then fiscal policy in Germany can reduce the loss to zero.

Table 3.8
Fiscal Policy in Germany
A Demand Shock

Unemployment	0	Inflation	0
Shock in A_1	1	Shock in B_1	-1
Unemployment	1	Inflation	-1
Change in Govt Purchases	1		
Unemployment	0	Inflation	0

2) A supply shock in Germany. Let initial unemployment and inflation in Germany be zero each. Step one refers to the supply shock in Germany. In terms of the model there is an increase in B_1 of 1 unit and an increase in A_1 of equally 1 unit. Step two refers to the outside lag. Inflation in Germany goes from zero to 1 percent. And unemployment there goes from zero to 1 percent as well. Step

three refers to the policy response. What is needed, according to the model, is to hold German government purchases constant. Step four refers to the outside lag. Obviously, inflation in Germany stays at 1 percent, as does unemployment there. Table 3.9 gives an overview.

As a result, given a supply shock in Germany, fiscal policy in Germany is ineffective. The supply shock in Germany causes a loss of 2 units. However, fiscal policy in Germany cannot reduce the loss.

Table 3.9
Fiscal Policy in Germany
A Supply Shock

Unemployment	0	Inflation	0
Shock in A_1	1	Shock in B_1	1
Unemployment	1	Inflation	1
Change in Govt Purchases	0		
Unemployment	1	Inflation	1

3) Summary. Given a demand shock in Germany, fiscal policy in Germany can achieve both zero unemployment and zero inflation. Given a supply shock in Germany, fiscal policy in Germany is ineffective. Given a mixed shock in Germany, fiscal policy in Germany can reduce the loss caused by unemployment and inflation. However, it cannot achieve zero unemployment and zero inflation.

4) Comparing cases A and B. As to the policy targets there are two distinct cases. In case A, by definition, the target of the German government is zero unemployment. In case B, by definition, the targets of the German government are zero unemployment and zero inflation. First consider a demand shock in Germany. In case A, given a demand shock, fiscal policy can achieve zero unemployment. And what is more, as a side effect, it can achieve zero inflation. In case B, given a demand shock, fiscal policy can achieve both zero

unemployment and zero inflation. Second consider a supply shock in Germany. In case A, given a supply shock, fiscal policy can achieve zero unemployment. However, as a side effect, it causes an increase in inflation. In case B, given a supply shock, fiscal policy is ineffective.

Chapter 5
Interaction between European Central Bank, German Government, and French Government

An increase in European money supply lowers unemployment in Germany and France. On the other hand, it raises inflation there. An increase in German government purchases lowers unemployment in Germany. On the other hand, it raises inflation there. Correspondingly, an increase in French government purchases lowers unemployment in France. On the other hand, it raises inflation there. The primary targets of the European central bank are zero inflation in Germany and France. The primary target of the German government is zero unemployment in Germany. And the primary target of the French government is zero unemployment in France.

The model of unemployment and inflation can be represented by a system of four equations:

$$u_1 = A_1 - M - G_1 \tag{1}$$

$$u_2 = A_2 - M - G_2 \tag{2}$$

$$\pi_1 = B_1 + M + G_1 \tag{3}$$

$$\pi_2 = B_2 + M + G_2 \tag{4}$$

Here u_1 denotes the rate of unemployment in Germany, u_2 is the rate of unemployment in France, π_1 is the rate of inflation in Germany, π_2 is the rate of inflation in France, M is European money supply, G_1 is German government purchases, G_2 is French government purchases, A_1 is some other factors bearing on the rate of unemployment in Germany, A_2 is some other factors bearing on the rate of unemployment in France, B_1 is some other factors bearing on the rate of inflation in Germany, and B_2 is some other factors bearing on the rate of inflation in France. The endogenous variables are the rate of unemployment in Germany, the rate of unemployment in France, the rate of inflation in Germany, and the rate of inflation in France.

According to equation (1), the rate of unemployment in Germany is a positive function of A_1, a negative function of European money supply, and a negative function of German government purchases. According to equation (2), the rate of unemployment in France is a positive function of A_2, a negative function of European money supply, and a negative function of French government purchases. According to equation (3), the rate of inflation in Germany is a positive function of B_1, a positive function of European money supply, and a positive function of German government purchases. According to equation (4), the rate of inflation in France is a positive function of B_2, a positive function of European money supply, and a positive function of French government purchases.

A unit increase in European money supply lowers the rates of unemployment in Germany and France by 1 percentage point each. On the other hand, it raises the rates of inflation there by 1 percentage point each. A unit increase in German government purchases lowers the rate of unemployment in Germany by 1 percentage point. On the other hand, it raises the rate of inflation there by 1 percentage point. Similarly, a unit increase in French government purchases lowers the rate of unemployment in France by 1 percentage point. On the other hand, it raises the rate of inflation there by 1 percentage point.

As to policy targets there are three distinct cases. In case A, the targets of the European central bank are zero inflation in Germany and France. The target of the German government is zero unemployment in Germany. And the target of the French government is zero unemployment in France. In case B, the targets of the European central bank are zero inflation and zero unemployment in each of the member countries. The target of the German government still is zero unemployment in Germany. And the target of the French government still is zero unemployment in France. In case C, the targets of the European central bank are zero inflation and zero unemployment in each of the member countries. The targets of the German government are zero unemployment and zero inflation in Germany. And the targets of the French government are zero unemployment and zero inflation in France.

1) Case A. The targets of the European central bank are zero inflation in Germany and France. The instrument of the European central bank is European money supply. There are two targets but only one instrument, so what is needed is a loss function. We assume that the European central bank has a quadratic loss function:

$$L = \pi_1^2 + \pi_2^2 \tag{5}$$

L is the loss to the European central bank caused by inflation in Germany and France. We assume equal weights in the loss function. The specific target of the European central bank is to minimize the loss, given the inflation functions. Taking account of equations (3) and (4), the loss function of the European central bank can be written as follows:

$$L = (B_1 + M + G_1)^2 + (B_2 + M + G_2)^2 \tag{6}$$

Then the first-order condition for a minimum loss gives the reaction function of the European central bank:

$$2M = -B_1 - B_2 - G_1 - G_2 \tag{7}$$

Suppose the German government raises German government purchases. Then, as a response, the European central bank lowers European money supply.

The target of the German government is zero unemployment in Germany. The instrument of the German government is German government purchases. By equation (1), the reaction function of the German government is:

$$G_1 = A_1 - M \tag{8}$$

Suppose the European central bank lowers European money supply. Then, as a response, the German government raises German government purchases.

The target of the French government is zero unemployment in France. The instrument of the French government is French government purchases. By equation (2), the reaction function of the French government is:

$$G_2 = A_2 - M \tag{9}$$

Suppose the European central bank lowers European money supply. Then, as a response, the French government raises French government purchases.

The Nash equilibrium is determined by the reaction functions of the European central bank, the German government, and the French government. From the reaction functions follows:

$$A_1 + A_2 + B_1 + B_2 = 0 \tag{10}$$

Evidently, this is in contradiction to the assumption that A_1, A_2, B_1 and B_2 are given exogenously. As an important result, in case A there is no Nash equilibrium.

2) Case B. The targets of the European central bank are zero inflation and zero unemployment in each of the member countries. The instrument of the European central bank is European money supply. There are four targets but only one instrument, so what is needed is a loss function. We assume that the European central bank has a quadratic loss function:

$$L = \pi_1^2 + \pi_2^2 + u_1^2 + u_2^2 \tag{11}$$

L is the loss to the European central bank caused by inflation and unemployment in each of the member countries. We assume equal weights in the loss function. The specific target of the European central bank is to minimize the loss, given the inflation functions and the unemployment functions. Taking account of equations (1), (2), (3) and (4), the loss function of the European central bank can be written as follows:

$$L = (B_1 + M + G_1)^2 + (B_2 + M + G_2)^2 \\ + (A_1 - M - G_1)^2 + (A_2 - M - G_2)^2 \tag{12}$$

Then the first-order condition for a minimum loss gives the reaction function of the European central bank:

$$4M = A_1 + A_2 - B_1 - B_2 - 2G_1 - 2G_2 \tag{13}$$

Suppose the German government raises German government purchases. Then, as a response, the European central bank lowers European money supply.

The target of the German government is zero unemployment in Germany. The instrument of the German government is German government purchases. By equation (1), the reaction function of the German government is:

$$G_1 = A_1 - M \tag{14}$$

Suppose the European central bank lowers European money supply. Then, as a response, the German government raises German government purchases.

The target of the French government is zero unemployment in France. The instrument of the French government is French government purchases. By equation (2), the reaction function of the French government is:

$$G_2 = A_2 - M \tag{15}$$

Suppose the European central bank lowers European money supply. Then, as a response, the French government raises French government purchases.

The Nash equilibrium is determined by the reaction functions of the European central bank, the German government, and the French government. From the reaction functions follows:

$$A_1 + A_2 + B_1 + B_2 = 0 \tag{16}$$

Obviously, this is in contradiction to the assumption that A_1, A_2, B_1 and B_2 are given exogenously. As an important result, in case B there is no Nash equilibrium.

3) Case C. The targets of the European central bank are zero inflation and zero unemployment in each of the member countries. The instrument of the European central bank is European money supply. There are four targets but only one instrument, so what is needed is a loss function. We assume that the European central bank has a quadratic loss function:

$$L = \pi_1^2 + \pi_2^2 + u_1^2 + u_2^2 \tag{17}$$

L is the loss to the European central bank caused by inflation and unemployment in each of the member countries. We assume equal weights in the loss function. The specific target of the European central bank is to minimize the loss, given the inflation functions and the unemployment functions. Taking account of equations (1), (2), (3) and (4), the loss function of the European central bank can be written as follows:

$$L = (B_1 + M + G_1)^2 + (B_2 + M + G_2)^2 \\ + (A_1 - M - G_1)^2 + (A_2 - M - G_2)^2 \tag{18}$$

Then the first-order condition for a minimum loss gives the reaction function of the European central bank:

$$4M = A_1 + A_2 - B_1 - B_2 - 2G_1 - 2G_2 \tag{19}$$

Suppose the German government raises German government purchases. Then, as a response, the European central bank lowers European money supply.

The targets of the German government are zero unemployment and zero inflation in Germany. The instrument of the German government is German government purchases. There are two targets but only one instrument, so what is needed is a loss function. We assume that the German government has a quadratic loss function:

$$L_1 = \pi_1^2 + u_1^2 \tag{20}$$

L_1 is the loss to the German government caused by inflation and unemployment in Germany. We assume equal weights in the loss function. The specific target of the German government is to minimize the loss, given the inflation function and the unemployment function. Taking account of equations (1) and (3), the loss function of the German government can be written as follows:

$$L_1 = (B_1 + M + G_1)^2 + (A_1 - M - G_1)^2 \qquad (21)$$

Then the first-order condition for a minimum loss gives the reaction function of the German government:

$$2G_1 = A_1 - B_1 - 2M \qquad (22)$$

Suppose the European central bank lowers European money supply. Then, as a response, the German government raises German government purchases.

The targets of the French government are zero unemployment and zero inflation in France. The instrument of the French government is French government purchases. There are two targets but only one instrument, so what is needed is a loss function. We assume that the French government has a quadratic loss function:

$$L_2 = \pi_2^2 + u_2^2 \qquad (23)$$

L_2 is the loss to the French government caused by inflation and unemployment in France. We assume equal weights in the loss function. The specific target of the French government is to minimize the loss, given the inflation function and the unemployment function. Taking account of equations (2) and (4), the loss function of the French government can be written as follows:

$$L_2 = (B_2 + M + G_2)^2 + (A_2 - M - G_2)^2 \qquad (24)$$

Then the first-order condition for a minimum loss gives the reaction function of the French government:

$$2G_2 = A_2 - B_2 - 2M \qquad (25)$$

Suppose the European central bank lowers European money supply. Then, as a response, the French government raises French government purchases.

The Nash equilibrium is determined by the reaction functions of the European central bank, the German government, and the French government:

$$4M = A_1 + A_2 - B_1 - B_2 - 2G_1 - 2G_2 \tag{26}$$

$$2G_1 = A_1 - B_1 - 2M \tag{27}$$

$$2G_2 = A_2 - B_2 - 2M \tag{28}$$

Now take the sum of equations (27) and (28) to find out:

$$4M = A_1 + A_2 - B_1 - B_2 - 2G_1 - 2G_2 \tag{29}$$

Clearly, equations (26) and (29) are identical. There are three endogenous variables (M, G_1, G_2). On the other hand, there are only two independent equations. As an important result, in case C there are multiple Nash equilibria.

4) Summary. In case A there is no Nash equilibrium. In case B there is no Nash equilibrium either. And in case C there are multiple Nash equilibria.

Chapter 6
Cooperation between European Central Bank, German Government, and French Government

1. The Model

An increase in European money supply lowers unemployment in Germany and France. On the other hand, it raises inflation there. An increase in German government purchases lowers unemployment in Germany. On the other hand, it raises inflation there. Correspondingly, an increase in French government purchases lowers unemployment in France. On the other hand, it raises inflation there. The policy makers are the European central bank, the German government, and the French government. The targets of policy cooperation are zero inflation and zero unemployment in each of the member countries.

The model of unemployment and inflation can be characterized by a system of four equations:

$$u_1 = A_1 - M - G_1 \tag{1}$$

$$u_2 = A_2 - M - G_2 \tag{2}$$

$$\pi_1 = B_1 + M + G_1 \tag{3}$$

$$\pi_2 = B_2 + M + G_2 \tag{4}$$

Here u_1 denotes the rate of unemployment in Germany, u_2 is the rate of unemployment in France, π_1 is the rate of inflation in Germany, π_2 is the rate of inflation in France, M is European money supply, G_1 is German government purchases, G_2 is French government purchases, A_1 is some other factors bearing on the rate of unemployment in Germany, A_2 is some other factors bearing on the rate of unemployment in France, B_1 is some other factors bearing on the rate of inflation in Germany, and B_2 is some other factors bearing on the rate of inflation in France. The endogenous variables are the rate of unemployment in Germany, the rate of unemployment in France, the rate of inflation in Germany, and the rate of inflation in France.

According to equation (1), the rate of unemployment in Germany is a positive function of A_1, a negative function of European money supply, and a negative function of German government purchases. According to equation (2), the rate of unemployment in France is a positive function of A_2, a negative function of European money supply, and a negative function of French government purchases. According to equation (3), the rate of inflation in Germany is a positive function of B_1, a positive function of European money supply, and a positive function of German government purchases. According to equation (4), the rate of inflation in France is a positive function of B_2, a positive function of European money supply, and a positive function of French government purchases.

A unit increase in European money supply lowers the rates of unemployment in Germany and France by 1 percentage point each. On the other hand, it raises the rates of inflation there by 1 percentage point each. A unit increase in German government purchases lowers the rate of unemployment in Germany by 1 percentage point. On the other hand, it raises the rate of inflation there by 1 percentage point. Similarly, a unit increase in French government purchases lowers the rate of unemployment in France by 1 percentage point. On the other hand, it raises the rate of inflation there by 1 percentage point.

The policy makers are the European central bank, the German government, and the French government. The targets of policy cooperation are zero inflation and zero unemployment in each of the member countries. The instruments of policy cooperation are European money supply, German government purchases, and French government purchases. There are four targets but only three instruments, so what is needed is a loss function. We assume that the policy makers agree on a common loss function:

$$L = \pi_1^2 + \pi_2^2 + u_1^2 + u_2^2 \tag{5}$$

L is the loss caused by inflation and unemployment in each of the member countries. We assume equal weights in the loss function. The specific target of policy cooperation is to minimize the loss, given the inflation functions and the unemployment functions. Taking account of equations (1), (2), (3) and (4), the loss function under policy cooperation can be written as follows:

$$L = (B_1 + M + G_1)^2 + (B_2 + M + G_2)^2$$
$$+ (A_1 - M - G_1)^2 + (A_2 - M - G_2)^2 \quad (6)$$

Then the first-order conditions for a minimum loss are:

$$4M = A_1 + A_2 - B_1 - B_2 - 2G_1 - 2G_2 \quad (7)$$
$$2G_1 = A_1 - B_1 - 2M \quad (8)$$
$$2G_2 = A_2 - B_2 - 2M \quad (9)$$

Equation (7) shows the first-order condition with respect to European money supply. Equation (8) shows the first-order condition with respect to German government purchases. And equation (9) shows the first-order condition with respect to French government purchases. Adding up equations (8) and (9) gives:

$$4M = A_1 + A_2 - B_1 - B_2 - 2G_1 - 2G_2 \quad (10)$$

Obviously, equations (7) and (10) are identical.

The cooperative equilibrium is determined by the first-order conditions for a minimum loss:

$$2M + 2G_1 = A_1 - B_1 \quad (11)$$
$$2M + 2G_2 = A_2 - B_2 \quad (12)$$

Equations (11) and (12) yield the optimum combinations of European money supply, German government purchases, and French government purchases. There are three endogenous variables. On the other hand, there are only two independent equations. Thus there is an infinite number of solutions. As a result, monetary and fiscal cooperation can reduce the loss caused by inflation and unemployment.

From equations (1) and (11) follows the optimum rate of unemployment in Germany:

$$2u_1 = A_1 + B_1 \tag{13}$$

And from equations (2) and (12) follows the optimum rate of unemployment in France:

$$2u_2 = A_2 + B_2 \tag{14}$$

By definition, the rate of unemployment in Europe is:

$$u = 0.5u_1 + 0.5u_2 \tag{15}$$

Making use of equations (13) and (14), the optimum rate of unemployment in Europe is:

$$4u = A_1 + A_2 + B_1 + B_2 \tag{16}$$

From equations (3) and (11) follows the optimum rate of inflation in Germany:

$$2\pi_1 = A_1 + B_1 \tag{17}$$

And from equations (4) and (12) follows the optimum rate of inflation in France:

$$2\pi_2 = A_2 + B_2 \tag{18}$$

By definition, the rate of inflation in Europe is:

$$\pi = 0.5\pi_1 + 0.5\pi_2 \tag{19}$$

Making use of equations (17) and (18), the optimum rate of inflation in Europe is:

$$4\pi = A_1 + A_2 + B_1 + B_2 \tag{20}$$

Unemployment in Germany, France and Europe is not zero, nor is inflation there.

2. Some Numerical Examples

For easy reference, the model of unemployment and inflation is reproduced here:

$$u_1 = A_1 - M - G_1 \tag{1}$$
$$u_2 = A_2 - M - G_2 \tag{2}$$
$$\pi_1 = B_1 + M + G_1 \tag{3}$$
$$\pi_2 = B_2 + M + G_2 \tag{4}$$

The optimum combinations of European money supply, German government purchases, and French government purchases are given by:

$$2M + 2G_1 = A_1 - B_1 \tag{5}$$
$$2M + 2G_2 = A_2 - B_2 \tag{6}$$

It proves useful to study three distinct cases:
- a demand shock in Germany
- a supply shock in Germany
- a mixed shock in Germany.

1) A demand shock in Germany. In each of the member countries, let initial unemployment be zero, and let initial inflation be zero as well. Step one refers to a decline in the demand for German goods. In terms of the model there is an increase in A_1 of 2 units and a decline in B_1 of equally 2 units. Step two refers to the outside lag. Unemployment in Germany goes from zero to 2 percent. Unemployment in France stays at zero percent. Inflation in Germany goes from zero to – 2 percent. And inflation in France stays at zero percent.

Step three refers to the policy response. According to the model, a first solution is an increase in European money supply of 1 unit, an increase in German government purchases of 1 unit, and a reduction in French government purchases of equally 1 unit. Step four refers to the outside lag. Unemployment in

Germany goes from 2 to zero percent. Unemployment in France stays at zero percent. Inflation in Germany goes from – 2 to zero percent. And inflation in France stays at zero percent. Table 3.10 presents a synopsis.

Table 3.10
Cooperation between European Central Bank,
German Government, and French Government
A Demand Shock in Germany

Germany		France	
Unemployment	0	Unemployment	0
Inflation	0	Inflation	0
Shock in A_1	2		
Shock in B_1	– 2		
Unemployment	2	Unemployment	0
Inflation	– 2	Inflation	0
Δ European Money Supply	1		
Δ Government Purchases	1	Δ Government Purchases	– 1
Unemployment	0	Unemployment	0
Inflation	0	Inflation	0

As a result, given a demand shock in Germany, monetary and fiscal cooperation can achieve zero inflation and zero unemployment in each of the member countries. A second solution is an increase in European money supply of 2 units, an increase in German government purchases of zero units, and a reduction in French government purchases of 2 units. A third solution is an increase in European money supply of zero units, an increase in German government purchases of 2 units, and a reduction in French government purchases of zero units. And so on. The loss function under policy cooperation is:

$$L = \pi_1^2 + \pi_2^2 + u_1^2 + u_2^2 \tag{7}$$

The initial loss is zero. The demand shock in Germany causes a loss of 8 units. Then policy cooperation can reduce the loss to zero.

2) A supply shock in Germany. In each of the member countries, let initial unemployment be zero, and let initial inflation be zero as well. Step one refers to the supply shock in Germany. In terms of the model there is an increase in B_1 of 2 units and an increase in A_1 of equally 2 units. Step two refers to the outside lag. Inflation in Germany goes from zero to 2 percent. Inflation in France stays at zero percent. Unemployment in Germany goes from zero to 2 percent. And unemployment in France stays at zero percent.

Step three refers to the policy response. According to the model, a first solution is to hold European money supply, German government purchases, and French government purchases constant. Step four refers to the outside lag. Inflation in Germany stays at 2 percent, and inflation in France stays at zero percent. Thus inflation in Europe stays at 1 percent. Unemployment in Germany stays at 2 percent, and unemployment in France stays at zero percent. Thus unemployment in Europe stays at 1 percent. Table 3.11 gives an overview.

As a result, given a supply shock in Germany, monetary and fiscal cooperation is ineffective. A second solution is an increase in European money supply of 1 unit, a reduction in German government purchases of 1 unit, and a reduction in French government purchases of equally 1 unit. And so on. The supply shock in Germany causes a loss of 8 units. However, policy cooperation cannot reduce the loss.

3) A mixed shock in Germany. In each of the member countries, let initial unemployment be zero, and let initial inflation be zero as well. Step one refers to the mixed shock in Germany. In terms of the model there is an increase in B_1 of 4 units. Step two refers to the outside lag. Inflation in Germany goes from zero to 4 percent. Inflation in France stays at zero percent. Unemployment in Germany stays at zero percent, as does unemployment in France.

Step three refers to the policy response. According to the model, a first solution is a reduction in European money supply of 1 unit, a reduction in

German government purchases of 1 unit, and an increase in French government purchases of equally 1 unit. Step four refers to the outside lag. Inflation in Germany goes from 4 to 2 percent. Inflation in France stays at zero percent. Unemployment in Germany goes from zero to 2 percent. And unemployment in France stays at zero percent. For a synopsis see Table 3.12.

As a result, given a mixed shock in Germany, monetary and fiscal cooperation can reduce the loss caused by inflation and unemployment. However, it cannot achieve zero inflation and zero unemployment in each of the member countries. The mixed shock in Germany causes a loss of 16 units. Then policy cooperation can reduce the loss to 8 units.

Table 3.11
Cooperation between European Central Bank,
German Government, and French Government
A Supply Shock in Germany

	Germany		France	
Unemployment	0	Unemployment	0
Inflation	0	Inflation	0
Shock in A_1	2		
Shock in B_1	2		
Unemployment	2	Unemployment	0
Inflation	2	Inflation	0
Δ European Money Supply	0		
Δ Government Purchases	0	Δ Government Purchases	0
Unemployment	2	Unemployment	0
Inflation	2	Inflation	0

Table 3.12
Cooperation between European Central Bank, German Government, and French Government
A Mixed Shock in Germany

Germany		France	
Unemployment	0	Unemployment	0
Inflation	0	Inflation	0
Shock in A_1	0		
Shock in B_1	4		
Unemployment	0	Unemployment	0
Inflation	4	Inflation	0
Δ European Money Supply	-1		
Δ Government Purchases	-1	Δ Government Purchases	1
Unemployment	2	Unemployment	0
Inflation	2	Inflation	0

4) Summary. Given a demand shock in Germany, policy cooperation can achieve zero inflation and zero unemployment in each of the member countries. Given a supply shock in Germany, policy cooperation is ineffective. Given a mixed shock in Germany, policy cooperation can reduce the loss caused by inflation and unemployment to a certain extent.

5) Comparing policy cooperation with policy interaction. Under policy interaction there is no unique Nash equilibrium. By contrast, policy cooperation can reduce the loss caused by inflation and unemployment. Judging from this point of view, policy cooperation seems to be superior to policy interaction.

Part Four

The Monetary Union of Two Countries

Presence of a Deficit Target

Chapter 1
Fiscal Policy in Germany A

1. The Model

The monetary union consists of two countries, say Germany and France. The member countries are the same size and have the same behavioural functions. An increase in German government purchases lowers unemployment in Germany. On the other hand, it raises inflation there. And what is more, it raises the structural deficit.

The model of unemployment, inflation, and the structural deficit can be represented by a system of three equations:

$$u_1 = A_1 - G_1 \tag{1}$$

$$\pi_1 = B_1 + G_1 \tag{2}$$

$$s_1 = G_1 - T_1 \tag{3}$$

Here u_1 denotes the rate of unemployment in Germany, π_1 is the rate of inflation in Germany, s_1 is the structural deficit in Germany, G_1 is German government purchases, T_1 is German tax revenue at full-employment output, $G_1 - T_1$ is the structural deficit in Germany, A_1 is some other factors bearing on the rate of unemployment in Germany, and B_1 is some other factors bearing on the rate of inflation in Germany. The endogenous variables are the rate of unemployment, the rate of inflation, and the structural deficit ratio.

According to equation (1), the rate of unemployment in Germany is a positive function of A_1 and a negative function of German government purchases. According to equation (2), the rate of inflation in Germany is a positive function of B_1 and a positive function of German government purchases. According to equation (3), the structural deficit ratio in Germany is a positive function of German government purchases.

A unit increase in government purchases lowers the rate of unemployment by 1 percentage point. On the other hand, it raises the rate of inflation by 1 percentage point. And what is more, it raises the structural deficit ratio by 1 percentage point. For instance, let initial unemployment be 2 percent, let initial inflation be 2 percent, and let the initial structural deficit be 2 percent as well. Now consider a unit increase in government purchases. Then unemployment goes from 2 to 1 percent. On the other hand, inflation goes from 2 to 3 percent. And what is more, the structural deficit goes from 2 to 3 percent as well.

As to policy targets there are two distinct cases. In case A the targets of the government are zero unemployment and a zero structural deficit. In case B the targets of the government are zero unemployment, zero inflation, and a zero structural deficit. This chapter deals with case A, and the next chapter deals with case B.

The targets of the German government are zero unemployment and a zero structural deficit in Germany. The instrument of the German government is German government purchases. There are two targets but only one instrument, so what is needed is a loss function. We assume that the German government has a quadratic loss function:

$$L_1 = u_1^2 + s_1^2 \tag{4}$$

L_1 is the loss to the German government caused by unemployment and the structural deficit. We assume equal weights in the loss function. The specific target of the German government is to minimize the loss, given the unemployment function and the structural deficit function. Taking account of equations (1) and (3), the loss function of the German government can be written as follows:

$$L_1 = (A_1 - G_1)^2 + (G_1 - T_1)^2 \tag{5}$$

Then the first-order condition for a minimum loss is:

$$2G_1 = A_1 + T_1 \tag{6}$$

Here G_1 is the optimum level of German government purchases. An increase in A_1 requires an increase in German government purchases. And an increase in B_1 requires no change in German government purchases. From equations (1) and (6) follows the optimum rate of unemployment in Germany:

$$2u_1 = A_1 - T_1 \qquad (7)$$

From equations (2) and (6) follows the optimum rate of inflation in Germany:

$$2\pi_1 = A_1 + 2B_1 + T_1 \qquad (8)$$

And from equations (3) and (6) follows the optimum structural deficit ratio:

$$2s_1 = A_1 - T_1 \qquad (9)$$

Unemployment in Germany is not zero. And the same holds for inflation and the structural deficit there.

2. Some Numerical Examples

For easy reference, the basic model is summarized here:

$$u_1 = A_1 - G_1 \qquad (1)$$
$$\pi_1 = B_1 + G_1 \qquad (2)$$
$$s_1 = G_1 - T_1 \qquad (3)$$

And the optimum level of German government purchases is:

$$2G_1 = A_1 + T_1 \qquad (4)$$

It proves useful to study two distinct cases:
- a demand shock in Germany
- a supply shock in Germany.

1) A demand shock in Germany. Let initial unemployment be zero, let initial inflation be zero, and let the initial structural deficit be zero as well. Step one refers to a decline in the demand for German goods. In terms of the model there is an increase in A_1 of 6 units and a decline in B_1 of equally 6 units. Step two refers to the outside lag. Unemployment goes from zero to 6 percent. Inflation goes from zero to -6 percent. And the structural deficit stays at zero percent. Step three refers to the policy response. What is needed, according to the model, is an increase in government purchases of 3 units. Step four refers to the outside lag. Unemployment goes from 6 to 3 percent. The structural deficit goes from zero to 3 percent. And inflation goes from -6 to -3 percent. Table 4.1 presents a synopsis.

Table 4.1
Fiscal Policy in Germany
A Demand Shock

Unemployment	0	Inflation	0
Structural Deficit	0		
Shock in A_1	6	Shock in B_1	-6
Unemployment	6	Inflation	-6
Structural Deficit	0		
Change in Govt Purchases	3		
Unemployment	3	Inflation	-3
Structural Deficit	3		

As a result, given a demand shock in Germany, fiscal policy in Germany can reduce the loss caused by unemployment and the structural deficit. However, it cannot achieve zero unemployment and a zero structural deficit. The loss function of the German government is:

$$L_1 = u_1^2 + s_1^2 \tag{5}$$

The initial loss is zero. The demand shock causes a loss of 36 units. Then fiscal policy can reduce the loss to 18 units.

2) A supply shock in Germany. Let initial unemployment be zero, let initial inflation be zero, and let the initial structural deficit be zero as well. Step one refers to the supply shock. In terms of the model there is an increase in B_1 of 6 units and an increase in A_1 of equally 6 units. Step two refers to the outside lag. Inflation goes from zero to 6 percent. Unemployment goes from zero to 6 percent as well. And the structural deficit stays at zero percent. Step three refers to the policy response. What is needed, according to the model, is an increase in government purchases of 3 units. Step four refers to the outside lag. Unemployment goes from 6 to 3 percent. The structural deficit goes from zero to 3 percent. And inflation goes from 6 to 9 percent. Table 4.2 gives an overview.

Table 4.2
Fiscal Policy in Germany
A Supply Shock

Unemployment	0	Inflation	0
Structural Deficit	0		
Shock in A_1	6	Shock in B_1	6
Unemployment	6	Inflation	6
Structural Deficit	0		
Change in Govt Purchases	3		
Unemployment	3	Inflation	9
Structural Deficit	3		

As a result, given a supply shock in Germany, fiscal policy in Germany can reduce the loss caused by unemployment and the structural deficit. However, it cannot achieve zero unemployment and a zero structural deficit. The supply shock causes a loss of 36 units. Then fiscal policy can reduce the loss to 18 units.

3) Summary. Given a demand shock in Germany, fiscal policy can reduce the loss to a certain extent. And the same is true of a supply shock in Germany.

Chapter 2
Fiscal Policy in Germany B

1. The Model

The model of unemployment, inflation, and the structural deficit can be characterized by a system of three equations:

$$u_1 = A_1 - G_1 \tag{1}$$

$$\pi_1 = B_1 + G_1 \tag{2}$$

$$s_1 = G_1 - T_1 \tag{3}$$

The targets of the German government are zero unemployment, zero inflation, and a zero structural deficit. The instrument of the German government is German government purchases. There are three targets but only one instrument, so what is needed is a loss function. We assume that the German government has a quadratic loss function:

$$L_1 = \pi_1^2 + u_1^2 + s_1^2 \tag{4}$$

L_1 is the loss to the German government caused by inflation, unemployment, and the structural deficit. We assume equal weights in the loss function. The specific target of the German government is to minimize the loss, given the inflation function, the unemployment function, and the structural deficit function. Taking account of equations (1), (2) and (3), the loss function of the German government can be written as follows:

$$L_1 = (B_1 + G_1)^2 + (A_1 - G_1)^2 + (G_1 - T_1)^2 \tag{5}$$

Then the first-order condition for a minimum loss is:

$$3G_1 = A_1 - B_1 + T_1 \tag{6}$$

Here G_1 is the optimum level of German government purchases. An increase in A_1 requires an increase in German government purchases. And an increase in B_1 requires a cut in German government purchases. From equations (1) and (6) follows the optimum rate of unemployment in Germany:

$$3u_1 = 2A_1 + B_1 - T_1 \tag{7}$$

From equations (2) and (6) follows the optimum rate of inflation in Germany:

$$3\pi_1 = A_1 + 2B_1 + T_1 \tag{8}$$

And from equations (3) and (6) follows the optimum structural deficit ratio:

$$3s_1 = A_1 - B_1 - 2T_1 \tag{9}$$

Unemployment in Germany is not zero. And the same holds for inflation and the structural deficit there.

2. Some Numerical Examples

For easy reference, the basic model is reproduced here:

$$u_1 = A_1 - G_1 \tag{1}$$
$$\pi_1 = B_1 + G_1 \tag{2}$$
$$s_1 = G_1 - T_1 \tag{3}$$

And the optimum level of German government purchases is:

$$3G_1 = A_1 - B_1 + T_1 \tag{4}$$

It proves useful to study two distinct cases:
- a demand shock in Germany
- a supply shock in Germany.

1) A demand shock in Germany. Let initial unemployment be zero, let initial inflation be zero, and let the initial structural deficit be zero as well. Step one refers to a decline in the demand for German goods. In terms of the model there is an increase in A_1 of 6 units and a decline in B_1 of equally 6 units. Step two refers to the outside lag. Unemployment goes from zero to 6 percent. Inflation goes from zero to − 6 percent. And the structural deficit stays at zero percent. Step three refers to the policy response. What is needed, according to the model, is an increase in government purchases of 4 units. Step four refers to the outside lag. Unemployment goes from 6 to 2 percent. Inflation goes from − 6 to − 2 percent. And the structural deficit goes from zero to 4 percent. Table 4.3 presents a synopsis.

Table 4.3
Fiscal Policy in Germany
A Demand Shock

Unemployment	0	Inflation	0
Structural Deficit	0		
Shock in A_1	6	Shock in B_1	− 6
Unemployment	6	Inflation	− 6
Structural Deficit	0		
Change in Govt Purchases	4		
Unemployment	2	Inflation	− 2
Structural Deficit	4		

As a result, given a demand shock in Germany, fiscal policy in Germany can reduce the loss caused by unemployment, inflation, and the structural deficit.

However, it cannot achieve zero unemployment, zero inflation, and a zero structural deficit. The loss function of the German government is:

$$L_1 = \pi_1^2 + u_1^2 + s_1^2 \tag{5}$$

The initial loss is zero. The demand shock causes a loss of 72 units. Then fiscal policy can reduce the loss to 24 units.

2) A supply shock in Germany. Let initial unemployment be zero, let initial inflation be zero, and let the initial structural deficit be zero as well. Step one refers to the supply shock. In terms of the model there is an increase in B_1 of 6 units and an increase in A_1 of equally 6 units. Step two refers to the outside lag. Inflation goes from zero to 6 percent. Unemployment goes from zero to 6 percent as well. And the structural deficit stays at zero percent. Step three refers to the policy response. What is needed, according to the model, is to hold government purchases constant. Step four refers to the outside lag. Obviously, inflation stays at 6 percent, unemployment stays at 6 percent, and the structural deficit stays at zero percent. Table 4.4 gives an overview.

Table 4.4
Fiscal Policy in Germany
A Supply Shock

Unemployment	0	Inflation	0
Structural Deficit	0		
Shock in A_1	6	Shock in B_1	6
Unemployment	6	Inflation	6
Structural Deficit	0		
Change in Govt Purchases	0		
Unemployment	6	Inflation	6
Structural Deficit	0		

As a result, given a supply shock in Germany, fiscal policy in Germany is ineffective. The supply shock causes a loss of 72 units. However, fiscal policy cannot reduce the loss.

3) Summary. Given a demand shock in Germany, fiscal policy can reduce the loss to a certain extent. Given a supply shock in Germany, fiscal policy is ineffective.

4) Comparing cases A and B. As to the policy targets there are two distinct cases. In case A, by definition, the targets of the government are zero unemployment and a zero structural deficit. In case B, by definition, the targets of the government are zero unemployment, zero inflation, and a zero structural deficit. First consider a demand shock. In case A, given a demand shock, fiscal policy can reduce the loss to a certain extent. In case B, given a demand shock, fiscal policy can reduce the loss to a greater extent. Second consider a supply shock. In case A, given a supply shock, fiscal policy can reduce the loss to a certain extent. In case B, given a supply shock, fiscal policy is ineffective.

Chapter 3
Interaction between European Central Bank, German Government, and French Government A

1. The Model

The monetary union consists of two countries, say Germany and France. The member countries are the same size and have the same behavioural functions. An increase in European money supply lowers unemployment in Germany and France. On the other hand, it raises inflation there. However, it has no effect on structural deficits. An increase in German government purchases lowers unemployment in Germany. On the other hand, it raises inflation there. And what is more, it raises the structural deficit. Correspondingly, an increase in French government purchases lowers unemployment in France. On the other hand, it raises inflation there. And what is more, it raises the structural deficit.

The primary targets of the European central bank are zero inflation in Germany and France respectively. The primary targets of the German government are zero unemployment and a zero structural deficit in Germany. And the primary targets of the French government are zero unemployment and a zero structural deficit in France.

The model of unemployment, inflation, and the structural deficit can be represented by a system of six equations:

$$u_1 = A_1 - M - G_1 \tag{1}$$

$$u_2 = A_2 - M - G_2 \tag{2}$$

$$\pi_1 = B_1 + M + G_1 \tag{3}$$

$$\pi_2 = B_2 + M + G_2 \tag{4}$$

$$s_1 = G_1 - T_1 \tag{5}$$

$$s_2 = G_2 - T_2 \tag{6}$$

Here u_1 denotes the rate of unemployment in Germany, u_2 is the rate of unemployment in France, π_1 is the rate of inflation in Germany, π_2 is the rate of inflation in France, s_1 is the structural deficit ratio in Germany, s_2 is the structural deficit ratio in France, M is European money supply, G_1 is German government purchases, G_2 is French government purchases, T_1 is German tax revenue at full-employment output, T_2 is French tax revenue at full-employment output, $G_1 - T_1$ is the structural deficit in Germany, $G_2 - T_2$ is the structural deficit in France, A_1 is some other factors bearing on the rate of unemployment in Germany, A_2 is some other factors bearing on the rate of unemployment in France, B_1 is some other factors bearing on the rate of inflation in Germany, and B_2 is some other factors bearing on the rate of inflation in France. The endogenous variables are the rates of unemployment, the rates of inflation, and the structural deficit ratios, in Germany and France respectively.

According to equation (1), the rate of unemployment in Germany is a positive function of A_1, a negative function of European money supply, and a negative function of German government purchases. According to equation (2), the rate of unemployment in France is a positive function of A_2, a negative function of European money supply, and a negative function of French government purchases. According to equation (3), the rate of inflation in Germany is a positive function of B_1, a positive function of European money supply, and a positive function of German government purchases. According to equation (4), the rate of inflation in France is a positive function of B_2, a positive function of European money supply, and a positive function of French government purchases. According to equation (5), the structural deficit ratio in Germany is a positive function of German government purchases. According to equation (6), the structural deficit ratio in France is a positive function of French government purchases.

A unit increase in European money supply lowers the rates of unemployment in Germany and France by 1 percentage point each. On the other hand, it raises the rates of inflation there by 1 percentage point each. However, it has no effect on the structural deficit ratios there. A unit increase in German government purchases lowers the rate of unemployment in Germany by 1 percentage point. On the other hand, it raises the rate of inflation there by 1 percentage point. And what is more, it raises the structural deficit ratio there by 1 percentage point as well. Similarly, a unit increase in French government purchases lowers the rate of unemployment in France by 1 percentage point. On the other hand, it raises the rate of inflation there by 1 percentage point. And what is more, it raises the structural deficit ratio there by 1 percentage point as well.

As to policy targets there are three distinct cases. In case A the targets of the European central bank are zero inflation in Germany and France. The targets of the German government are zero unemployment and a zero structural deficit in Germany. And the targets of the French government are zero unemployment and a zero structural deficit in France. In case B the targets of the European central bank are zero inflation and zero unemployment in each of the member countries. The targets of the German government still are zero unemployment and a zero structural deficit in Germany. And the targets of the French government still are zero unemployment and a zero structural deficit in France. In case C the targets of the European central bank are zero inflation and zero unemployment in each of the member countries. The targets of the German government are zero unemployment, zero inflation, and a zero structural deficit, in Germany respectively. And the targets of the French government are zero unemployment, zero inflation, and a zero structural deficit, in France respectively. This chapter deals with case A, and the next chapters deal with cases B and C.

The targets of the European central bank are zero inflation in Germany and France. The instrument of the European central bank is European money supply. There are two targets but only one instrument, so what is needed is a loss function. We assume that the European central bank has a quadratic loss function:

$$L = \pi_1^2 + \pi_2^2 \tag{7}$$

L is the loss to the European central bank caused by inflation in Germany and France. We assume equal weights in the loss function. The specific target of the European central bank is to minimize the loss, given the inflation functions. Taking account of equations (3) and (4), the loss function of the European central bank can be written as follows:

$$L = (B_1 + M + G_1)^2 + (B_2 + M + G_2)^2 \tag{8}$$

Then the first-order condition for a minimum loss gives the reaction function of the European central bank:

$$2M = -B_1 - B_2 - G_1 - G_2 \tag{9}$$

Suppose the German government raises German government purchases. Then, as a response, the European central bank lowers European money supply.

The targets of the German government are zero unemployment and a zero structural deficit in Germany. The instrument of the German government is German government purchases. There are two targets but only one instrument, so what is needed is a loss function. We assume that the German government has a quadratic loss function:

$$L_1 = u_1^2 + s_1^2 \tag{10}$$

L_1 is the loss to the German government caused by unemployment and the structural deficit in Germany. We assume equal weights in the loss function. The specific target of the German government is to minimize the loss, given the unemployment function and the structural deficit function. Taking account of equations (1) and (5), the loss function of the German government can be written as follows:

$$L_1 = (A_1 - M - G_1)^2 + (G_1 - T_1)^2 \tag{11}$$

Then the first-order condition for a minimum loss gives the reaction function of the German government:

$$2G_1 = A_1 + T_1 - M \tag{12}$$

Suppose the European central bank lowers European money supply. Then, as a response, the German government raises German government purchases.

The targets of the French government are zero unemployment and a zero structural deficit in France. The instrument of the French government is French government purchases. There are two targets but only one instrument, so what is needed is a loss function. We assume that the French government has a quadratic loss function:

$$L_2 = u_2^2 + s_2^2 \tag{13}$$

L_2 is the loss to the French government caused by unemployment and the structural deficit in France. We assume equal weights in the loss function. The specific target of the French government is to minimize the loss, given the unemployment function and the structural deficit function. Taking account of equations (2) and (6), the loss function of the French government can be written as follows:

$$L_2 = (A_2 - M - G_2)^2 + (G_2 - T_2)^2 \tag{14}$$

Then the first-order condition for a minimum loss gives the reaction function of the French government:

$$2G_2 = A_2 + T_2 - M \tag{15}$$

Suppose the European central bank lowers European money supply. Then, as a response, the French government raises French government purchases.

The Nash equilibrium is determined by the reaction functions of the European central bank, the German government, and the French government. We assume $T = T_1 = T_2$. The solution to this problem is as follows:

$$2M = -A_1 - A_2 - 2B_1 - 2B_2 - 2T \tag{16}$$

$$4G_1 = 3A_1 + A_2 + 2B_1 + 2B_2 + 4T \tag{17}$$

$$4G_2 = A_1 + 3A_2 + 2B_1 + 2B_2 + 4T \tag{18}$$

Equations (16), (17) and (18) show the Nash equilibrium of European money supply, German government purchases, and French government purchases. As a result, there is a unique Nash equilibrium.

According to equations (16), (17) and (18), an increase in A_1 causes a reduction in European money supply, an increase in German government purchases, and an increase in French government purchases. And an increase in B_1 has much the same effects. A unit increase in A_1 causes a reduction in European money supply of 0.5 units, an increase in German government purchases of 0.75 units, and an increase in French government purchases of 0.25 units. A unit increase in B_1 causes a reduction in European money supply of 1 unit, an increase in German government purchases of 0.5 units, and an increase in French government purchases of equally 0.5 units.

From equations (1), (16) and (17) follows the equilibrium rate of unemployment in Germany:

$$4u_1 = 3A_1 + A_2 + 2B_1 + 2B_2 \tag{19}$$

And from equations (2), (16) and (18) follows the equilibrium rate of unemployment in France:

$$4u_2 = A_1 + 3A_2 + 2B_1 + 2B_2 \tag{20}$$

By definition, the rate of unemployment in Europe is:

$$u = 0.5u_1 + 0.5u_2 \tag{21}$$

Making use of equations (19) and (20), the equilibrium rate of unemployment in Europe is:

$$2u = A_1 + A_2 + B_1 + B_2 \tag{22}$$

From equations (3), (16) and (17) follows the equilibrium rate of inflation in Germany:

$$4\pi_1 = A_1 - A_2 + 2B_1 - 2B_2 \tag{23}$$

And from equations (4), (16) and (18) follows the equilibrium rate of inflation in France:

$$4\pi_2 = A_2 - A_1 + 2B_2 - 2B_1 \tag{24}$$

By definition, the rate of inflation in Europe is:

$$\pi = 0.5\pi_1 + 0.5\pi_2 \tag{25}$$

Making use of equations (23) and (24), the equilibrium rate of inflation in Europe is:

$$\pi = 0 \tag{26}$$

From equations (5) and (17) follows the equilibrium structural deficit ratio in Germany:

$$4s_1 = 3A_1 + A_2 + 2B_1 + 2B_2 \tag{27}$$

And from equations (6) and (18) follows the equilibrium structural deficit ratio in France:

$$4s_2 = A_1 + 3A_2 + 2B_1 + 2B_2 \tag{28}$$

By definition, the structural deficit ratio in Europe is:

$$s = 0.5s_1 + 0.5s_2 \tag{29}$$

Making use of equations (27) and (28), the equilibrium structural deficit ratio in Europe is:

$$2s = A_1 + A_2 + B_1 + B_2 \tag{30}$$

Inflation in Europe is zero. However, inflation in Germany and France is not zero. Unemployment in Europe is not zero, nor is the structural deficit there.

2. Some Numerical Examples

For easy reference, the basic model is summarized here:

$$u_1 = A_1 - M - G_1 \tag{1}$$

$$u_2 = A_2 - M - G_2 \tag{2}$$

$$\pi_1 = B_1 + M + G_1 \tag{3}$$

$$\pi_2 = B_2 + M + G_2 \tag{4}$$

$$s_1 = G_1 - T_1 \tag{5}$$

$$s_2 = G_2 - T_2 \tag{6}$$

And the Nash equilibrium can be described by three equations:

$$2M = -A_1 - A_2 - 2B_1 - 2B_2 - 2T \tag{7}$$

$$4G_1 = 3A_1 + A_2 + 2B_1 + 2B_2 + 4T \tag{8}$$

$$4G_2 = A_1 + 3A_2 + 2B_1 + 2B_2 + 4T \tag{9}$$

It proves useful to study four distinct cases:
- a demand shock in Germany
- a supply shock in Germany
- a common demand shock in Europe
- a common supply shock in Europe.

1) A demand shock in Germany. In each of the member countries let initial unemployment be zero, let initial inflation be zero, and let the initial structural deficit be zero as well. Step one refers to a decline in the demand for German goods. In terms of the model there is an increase in A_1 of 12 units and a decline in B_1 of equally 12 units. Step two refers to the outside lag. Unemployment in Germany goes from zero to 12 percent. Unemployment in France stays at zero percent. Inflation in Germany goes from zero to − 12 percent. Inflation in France

stays at zero percent. The structural deficit in Germany stays at zero percent, as does the structural deficit in France.

Step three refers to the policy response. According to the Nash equilibrium there is an increase in European money supply of 6 units, an increase in German government purchases of 3 units, and a reduction in French government purchases of equally 3 units. Step four refers to the outside lag. Unemployment in Germany goes from 12 to 3 percent. Unemployment in France goes from zero to − 3 percent. Thus unemployment in Europe goes from 6 to zero percent. Inflation in Germany goes from − 12 to − 3 percent. Inflation in France goes from zero to 3 percent. Thus inflation in Europe goes from − 6 to zero percent. The structural deficit in Germany goes from zero to 3 percent. The structural deficit in France goes from zero to − 3 percent. Thus the structural deficit in Europe stays at zero percent. Table 4.5 presents a synopsis.

As a result, given a demand shock in Germany, monetary and fiscal interaction can achieve zero inflation, zero unemployment, and a zero structural deficit in Europe as a whole. However, it cannot do so in Germany and France.

The loss functions of the European central bank, the German government, and the French government are respectively:

$$L = \pi_1^2 + \pi_2^2 \tag{10}$$
$$L_1 = u_1^2 + s_1^2 \tag{11}$$
$$L_2 = u_2^2 + s_2^2 \tag{12}$$

The initial loss of the European central bank, the German government, and the French government is zero each. The demand shock in Germany causes a loss to the European central bank of 144 units, a loss to the German government of equally 144 units, and a loss to the French government of zero units. Then policy interaction reduces the loss of the European central bank from 144 to 18 units. And what is more, it reduces the loss of the German government from 144 to 18 units as well. On the other hand, it increases the loss of the French government from zero to 18 units.

Table 4.5
Interaction between European Central Bank,
German Government, and French Government
A Demand Shock in Germany

Germany		France	
Unemployment	0	Unemployment	0
Inflation	0	Inflation	0
Structural Deficit	0	Structural Deficit	0
Shock in A_1	12		
Shock in B_1	-12		
Unemployment	12	Unemployment	0
Inflation	-12	Inflation	0
Δ European Money Supply	6		
Δ Government Purchases	3	Δ Government Purchases	-3
Unemployment	3	Unemployment	-3
Inflation	-3	Inflation	3
Structural Deficit	3	Structural Deficit	-3

2) A supply shock in Germany. In each of the member countries let initial unemployment be zero, let initial inflation be zero, and let the initial structural deficit be zero as well. Step one refers to the supply shock in Germany. In terms of the model there is an increase in B_1 of 12 units and an increase in A_1 of equally 12 units. Step two refers to the outside lag. Inflation in Germany goes from zero to 12 percent. Inflation in France stays at zero percent. Unemployment in Germany goes from zero to 12 percent. And unemployment in France stays at zero percent.

Step three refers to the policy response. According to the Nash equilibrium there is a reduction in European money supply of 18 units, an increase in German government purchases of 15 units, and an increase in French government

purchases of 9 units. Step four refers to the outside lag. Inflation in Germany goes from 12 to 9 percent. Inflation in France goes from zero to − 9 percent. Thus inflation in Europe goes from 6 to zero percent. Unemployment in Germany goes from 12 to 15 percent. Unemployment in France goes from zero to 9 percent. Thus unemployment in Europe goes from 6 to 12 percent. The structural deficit in Germany goes from zero to 15 percent. The structural deficit in France goes from zero to 9 percent. Thus the structural deficit in Europe goes from zero to 12 percent. Table 4.6 gives an overview.

As a result, given a supply shock in Germany, monetary and fiscal interaction can achieve zero inflation in Europe as a whole. On the other hand, it causes an increase in both unemployment and the structural deficit.

Table 4.6
Interaction between European Central Bank,
German Government, and French Government
A Supply Shock in Germany

Germany		France	
Unemployment	0	Unemployment	0
Inflation	0	Inflation	0
Structural Deficit	0	Structural Deficit	0
Shock in A_1	12		
Shock in B_1	12		
Unemployment	12	Unemployment	0
Inflation	12	Inflation	0
Δ European Money Supply − 18			
Δ Government Purchases	15	Δ Government Purchases	9
Unemployment	15	Unemployment	9
Inflation	9	Inflation	− 9
Structural Deficit	15	Structural Deficit	9

The supply shock in Germany causes a loss to the European central bank of 144 units, a loss to the German government of equally 144 units, and a loss to the French government of zero units. Then policy interaction increases the loss of the European central bank from 144 to 162 units. It increases the loss of the German government from 144 to 450 units. And it increases the loss of the French government from zero to 162 units. To sum up, policy interaction increases the total loss from 288 to 774 units. In other words, the Nash equilibrium seems to be Pareto inefficient.

3) A common demand shock in Europe. In each of the member countries let initial unemployment be zero, let initial inflation be zero, and let the initial structural deficit be zero as well. Step one refers to a decline in the common demand for European goods. In terms of the model there is an increase in A_1 of 12 units, an increase in A_2 of 12 units, a decline in B_1 of 12 units, and a decline in B_2 of equally 12 units. Step two refers to the outside lag. Unemployment in Germany goes from zero to 12 percent, as does unemployment in France. Inflation in Germany goes from zero to -12 percent, as does inflation in France.

Step three refers to the policy response. According to the Nash equilibrium there is an increase in European money supply of 12 units, an increase in German government purchases of zero units, and an increase in French government purchases of equally zero units. Step four refers to the outside lag. Unemployment in Germany goes from 12 to zero percent, as does unemployment in France. Inflation in Germany goes from -12 to zero percent, as does inflation in France. The structural deficit in Germany stays at zero percent, as does the structural deficit in France. For a synopsis see Table 4.7.

As a result, given a common demand shock in Europe, monetary and fiscal interaction can achieve zero inflation, zero unemployment, and a zero structural deficit in each of the member countries.

Table 4.7
Interaction between European Central Bank,
German Government, and French Government
A Common Demand Shock in Europe

Germany		France	
Unemployment	0	Unemployment	0
Inflation	0	Inflation	0
Structural Deficit	0	Structural Deficit	0
Shock in A_1	12	Shock in A_2	12
Shock in B_1	-12	Shock in B_2	-12
Unemployment	12	Unemployment	12
Inflation	-12	Inflation	-12
Δ European Money Supply	12		
Δ Government Purchases	0	Δ Government Purchases	0
Unemployment	0	Unemployment	0
Inflation	0	Inflation	0
Structural Deficit	0	Structural Deficit	0

4) A common supply shock in Europe. In each of the member countries let initial unemployment be zero, let initial inflation be zero, and let the initial structural deficit be zero as well. Step one refers to the common supply shock in Europe. In terms of the model there is an increase in B_1 of 12 units, an increase in B_2 of 12 units, an increase in A_1 of 12 units, and an increase in A_2 of equally 12 units. Step two refers to the outside lag. Inflation in Germany goes from zero to 12 percent, as does inflation in France. Unemployment in Germany goes from zero to 12 percent, as does unemployment in France.

Step three refers to the policy response. According to the Nash equilibrium there is a reduction in European money supply of 36 units, an increase in German government purchases of 24 units, and an increase in French government

purchases of equally 24 units. Step four refers to the outside lag. Inflation in Germany goes from 12 to zero percent, as does inflation in France. Unemployment in Germany goes from 12 to 24 percent, as does unemployment in France. The structural deficit in Germany goes from zero to 24 percent, as does the structural deficit in France. For an overview see Table 4.8.

As a result, given a common supply shock in Europe, monetary and fiscal interaction can achieve zero inflation in each of the member countries. On the other hand, it causes an increase in both unemployment and the structural deficit.

The common supply shock in Europe causes a loss to the European central bank of 288 units, a loss to the German government of 144 units, and a loss to the French government of equally 144 units. Then policy interaction reduces the loss of the European central bank from 288 to zero units. On the other hand, it increases the loss of the German government from 144 to 1152 units. And it increases the loss of the French government from 144 to equally 1152 units. To sum up, policy interaction increases the total loss from 576 to 2304.

5) Summary. Given a demand shock in Germany, policy interaction can achieve zero inflation, zero unemployment, and a zero structural deficit in Europe as a whole. However, it cannot do so in Germany and France. Given a supply shock in Germany, policy interaction can achieve zero inflation in Europe as a whole. On the other hand, it causes an increase in both unemployment and the structural deficit. Given a common demand shock in Europe, policy interaction can achieve zero inflation, zero unemployment, and a zero structural deficit in each of the member countries. Given a common supply shock in Europe, policy interaction can achieve zero inflation in each of the member countries. On the other hand, it causes an increase in both unemployment and the structural deficit.

Table 4.8
**Interaction between European Central Bank,
German Government, and French Government**
A Common Supply Shock in Europe

Germany		France	
Unemployment	0	Unemployment	0
Inflation	0	Inflation	0
Structural Deficit	0	Structural Deficit	0
Shock in A_1	12	Shock in A_2	12
Shock in B_1	12	Shock in B_2	12
Unemployment	12	Unemployment	12
Inflation	12	Inflation	12
Δ European Money Supply -36			
Δ Government Purchases	24	Δ Government Purchases	24
Unemployment	24	Unemployment	24
Inflation	0	Inflation	0
Structural Deficit	24	Structural Deficit	24

Chapter 4
Interaction between European Central Bank, German Government, and French Government B

1. The Model

This chapter deals with case B. The targets of the European central bank are zero inflation and zero unemployment in each of the member countries. The targets of the German government are zero unemployment and a zero structural deficit in Germany. And the targets of the French government are zero unemployment and a zero structural deficit in France.

The model of unemployment, inflation, and the structural deficit can be characterized by a system of six equations:

$$u_1 = A_1 - M - G_1 \tag{1}$$

$$u_2 = A_2 - M - G_2 \tag{2}$$

$$\pi_1 = B_1 + M + G_1 \tag{3}$$

$$\pi_2 = B_2 + M + G_2 \tag{4}$$

$$s_1 = G_1 - T_1 \tag{5}$$

$$s_2 = G_2 - T_2 \tag{6}$$

The targets of the European central bank are zero inflation and zero unemployment in each of the member countries. The instrument of the European central bank is European money supply. There are four targets but only one instrument, so what is needed is a loss function. We assume that the European central bank has a quadratic loss function:

$$L = \pi_1^2 + \pi_2^2 + u_1^2 + u_2^2 \tag{7}$$

L is the loss to the European central bank caused by inflation and unemployment in each of the member countries. We assume equal weights in the loss function. The specific target of the European central bank is to minimize the loss, given the inflation functions and the unemployment functions. Taking account of equations (1) to (4), the loss function of the European central bank can be written as follows:

$$L = (B_1 + M + G_1)^2 + (B_2 + M + G_2)^2 \\ + (A_1 - M - G_1)^2 + (A_2 - M - G_2)^2 \tag{8}$$

Then the first-order condition for a minimum loss gives the reaction function of the European central bank:

$$4M = A_1 + A_2 - B_1 - B_2 - 2G_1 - 2G_2 \tag{9}$$

Suppose the German government raises German government purchases. Then, as a response, the European central bank lowers European money supply.

The targets of the German government are zero unemployment and a zero structural deficit in Germany. The instrument of the German government is German government purchases. There are two targets but only one instrument, so what is needed is a loss function. We assume that the German government has a quadratic loss function:

$$L_1 = u_1^2 + s_1^2 \tag{10}$$

L_1 is the loss to the German government caused by unemployment and the structural deficit in Germany. We assume equal weights in the loss function. The specific target of the German government is to minimize the loss, given the unemployment function and the structural deficit function. Taking account of equations (1) and (5), the loss function of the German government can be written as follows:

$$L_1 = (A_1 - M - G_1)^2 + (G_1 - T_1)^2 \tag{11}$$

Then the first-order condition for a minimum loss gives the reaction function of the German government:

$$2G_1 = A_1 + T_1 - M \tag{12}$$

Suppose the European central bank lowers European money supply. Then, as a response, the German government raises German government purchases.

The targets of the French government are zero unemployment and a zero structural deficit in France. The instrument of the French government is French government purchases. There are two targets but only one instrument, so what is needed is a loss function. We assume that the French government has a quadratic loss function:

$$L_2 = u_2^2 + s_2^2 \tag{13}$$

L_2 is the loss to the French government caused by unemployment and the structural deficit in France. We assume equal weights in the loss function. The specific target of the French government is to minimize the loss, given the unemployment function and the structural deficit function. Taking account of equations (2) and (6), the loss function of the French government can be written as follows:

$$L_2 = (A_2 - M - G_2)^2 + (G_2 - T_2)^2 \tag{14}$$

Then the first-order condition for a minimum loss gives the reaction function of the French government:

$$2G_2 = A_2 + T_2 - M \tag{15}$$

Suppose the European central bank lowers European money supply. Then, as a response, the French government raises French government purchases.

The Nash equilibrium is determined by the reaction functions of the European central bank, the German government, and the French government. We assume $T = T_1 = T_2$. The solution to this problem is as follows:

$$2M = -B_1 - B_2 - 2T \tag{16}$$

$$4G_1 = 2A_1 + B_1 + B_2 + 4T \tag{17}$$

$$4G_2 = 2A_2 + B_1 + B_2 + 4T \tag{18}$$

Equations (16), (17) and (18) show the Nash equilibrium of European money supply, German government purchases, and French government purchases. As a result, there is a unique Nash equilibrium. According to equations (16), (17) and (18), an increase in A_1 causes an increase in German government purchases. And an increase in B_1 causes a reduction in European money supply, an increase in German government purchases, and an increase in French government purchases.

From equations (1), (16) and (17) follows the equilibrium rate of unemployment in Germany:

$$4u_1 = 2A_1 + B_1 + B_2 \tag{19}$$

And from equations (2), (16) and (18) follows the equilibrium rate of unemployment in France:

$$4u_2 = 2A_2 + B_1 + B_2 \tag{20}$$

By definition, the rate of unemployment in Europe is:

$$u = 0.5u_1 + 0.5u_2 \tag{21}$$

Making use of equations (19) and (20), the equilibrium rate of unemployment in Europe is:

$$4u = A_1 + A_2 + B_1 + B_2 \tag{22}$$

From equations (3), (16) and (17) follows the equilibrium rate of inflation in Germany:

$$4\pi_1 = 2A_1 + 3B_1 - B_2 \tag{23}$$

And from equations (4), (16) and (18) follows the equilibrium rate of inflation in France:

$$4\pi_2 = 2A_2 - B_1 + 3B_2 \tag{24}$$

By definition, the rate of inflation in Europe is:

$$\pi = 0.5\pi_1 + 0.5\pi_2 \tag{25}$$

Making use of equations (23) and (24), the equilibrium rate of inflation in Europe is:

$$4\pi = A_1 + A_2 + B_1 + B_2 \tag{26}$$

From equations (5) and (17) follows the equilibrium structural deficit ratio in Germany:

$$4s_1 = 2A_1 + B_1 + B_2 \tag{27}$$

And from equations (6) and (18) follows the equilibrium structural deficit ratio in France:

$$4s_2 = 2A_2 + B_1 + B_2 \tag{28}$$

By definition, the structural deficit ratio in Europe is:

$$s = 0.5s_1 + 0.5s_2 \tag{29}$$

Making use of equations (27) and (28), the equilibrium structural deficit ratio in Europe is:

$$4s = A_1 + A_2 + B_1 + B_2 \tag{30}$$

Unemployment in Germany, France and Europe is not zero. And the same applies to inflation and the structural deficit there.

2. Some Numerical Examples

For easy reference, the basic model is reproduced here:

$$u_1 = A_1 - M - G_1 \tag{1}$$

$$u_2 = A_2 - M - G_2 \tag{2}$$

$$\pi_1 = B_1 + M + G_1 \tag{3}$$

$$\pi_2 = B_2 + M + G_2 \tag{4}$$

$$s_1 = G_1 - T_1 \tag{5}$$

$$s_2 = G_2 - T_2 \tag{6}$$

And the Nash equilibrium can be described by three equations:

$$2M = -B_1 - B_2 - 2T \tag{7}$$

$$4G_1 = 2A_1 + B_1 + B_2 + 4T \tag{8}$$

$$4G_2 = 2A_2 + B_1 + B_2 + 4T \tag{9}$$

It proves useful to study four distinct cases:
- a demand shock in Germany
- a supply shock in Germany
- a common demand shock in Europe
- a common supply shock in Europe.

1) A demand shock in Germany. In each of the member countries let initial unemployment be zero, let initial inflation be zero, and let the initial structural deficit be zero as well. Step one refers to a decline in the demand for German goods. In terms of the model there is an increase in A_1 of 12 units and a decline in B_1 of equally 12 units. Step two refers to the outside lag. Unemployment in Germany goes from zero to 12 percent. Unemployment in France stays at zero percent. Inflation in Germany goes from zero to − 12 percent. Inflation in France

stays at zero percent. The structural deficit in Germany stays at zero percent, as does the structural deficit in France.

Step three refers to the policy response. According to the Nash equilibrium there is an increase in European money supply of 6 units, an increase in German government purchases of 3 units, and a reduction in French government purchases of equally 3 units. Step four refers to the outside lag. Unemployment in Germany goes from 12 to 3 percent. Unemployment in France goes from zero to − 3 percent. Thus unemployment in Europe goes from 6 to zero percent. Inflation in Germany goes from − 12 to − 3 percent. Inflation in France goes from zero to 3 percent. Thus inflation in Europe goes from − 6 to zero percent. The structural deficit in Germany goes from zero to 3 percent. The structural deficit in France goes from zero to − 3 percent. Thus the structural deficit in Europe stays at zero percent. Table 4.9 presents a synopsis.

As a result, given a demand shock in Germany, monetary and fiscal interaction can achieve zero inflation, zero unemployment, and a zero structural deficit in Europe as a whole. However, it cannot do so in Germany and France.

The loss functions of the European central bank, the German government, and the French government are respectively:

$$L = \pi_1^2 + \pi_2^2 + u_1^2 + u_2^2 \qquad (10)$$
$$L_1 = u_1^2 + s_1^2 \qquad (11)$$
$$L_2 = u_2^2 + s_2^2 \qquad (12)$$

The initial loss of the European central bank, the German government, and the French government is zero each. The demand shock in Germany causes a loss to the European central bank of 288 units, a loss to the German government of 144 units, and a loss to the French government of zero units. Then policy interaction reduces the loss of the European central bank from 288 to 36 units. And what is more, it reduces the loss of the German government from 144 to 18 units. On the other hand, it increases the loss of the French government from zero to 18 units.

Table 4.9
Interaction between European Central Bank,
German Government, and French Government
A Demand Shock in Germany

Germany		France	
Unemployment	0	Unemployment	0
Inflation	0	Inflation	0
Structural Deficit	0	Structural Deficit	0
Shock in A_1	12		
Shock in B_1	− 12		
Unemployment	12	Unemployment	0
Inflation	− 12	Inflation	0
Δ European Money Supply	6		
Δ Government Purchases	3	Δ Government Purchases	− 3
Unemployment	3	Unemployment	− 3
Inflation	− 3	Inflation	3
Structural Deficit	3	Structural Deficit	− 3

2) A supply shock in Germany. In each of the member countries let initial unemployment be zero, let initial inflation be zero, and let the initial structural deficit be zero as well. Step one refers to the supply shock in Germany. In terms of the model there is an increase in B_1 of 12 units and an increase in A_1 of equally 12 units. Step two refers to the outside lag. Inflation in Germany goes from zero to 12 percent. Inflation in France stays at zero percent. Unemployment in Germany goes from zero to 12 percent. And unemployment in France stays at zero percent.

Step three refers to the policy response. According to the Nash equilibrium there is a reduction in European money supply of 6 units, an increase in German government purchases of 9 units, and an increase in French government

purchases of 3 units. Step four refers to the outside lag. Inflation in Germany goes from 12 to 15 percent. Inflation in France goes from zero to − 3 percent. Thus inflation in Europe stays at 6 percent. Unemployment in Germany goes from 12 to 9 percent. Unemployment in France goes from zero to 3 percent. Thus unemployment in Europe stays at 6 percent. The structural deficit in Germany goes from zero to 9 percent. The structural deficit in France goes from zero to 3 percent. Thus the structural deficit in Europe goes from zero to 6 percent. Table 4.10 gives an overview.

As a result, given a supply shock in Germany, monetary and fiscal interaction has no effect on inflation and unemployment in Europe as a whole. And what is more, it causes an increase in the structural deficit there.

Table 4.10
Interaction between European Central Bank,
German Government, and French Government
A Supply Shock in Germany

Germany		France	
Unemployment	0	Unemployment	0
Inflation	0	Inflation	0
Structural Deficit	0	Structural Deficit	0
Shock in A_1	12		
Shock in B_1	12		
Unemployment	12	Unemployment	0
Inflation	12	Inflation	0
Δ European Money Supply	− 6		
Δ Government Purchases	9	Δ Government Purchases	3
Unemployment	9	Unemployment	3
Inflation	15	Inflation	− 3
Structural Deficit	9	Structural Deficit	3

The supply shock in Germany causes a loss to the European central bank of 288 units, a loss to the German government of 144 units, and a loss to the French government of zero units. Then policy interaction increases the loss of the European central bank from 288 to 324 units. It increases the loss of the German government from 144 to 162 units. And it increases the loss of the French government from zero to 18 units. To sum up, policy interaction increases the total loss from 432 to 504 units. In other words, the Nash equilibrium seems to be Pareto inefficient.

3) A common demand shock in Europe. In each of the member countries let initial unemployment be zero, let initial inflation be zero, and let the initial structural deficit be zero as well. Step one refers to a decline in the common demand for European goods. In terms of the model there is an increase in A_1 of 12 units, an increase in A_2 of 12 units, a decline in B_1 of 12 units, and a decline in B_2 of equally 12 units. Step two refers to the outside lag. Unemployment in Germany goes from zero to 12 percent, as does unemployment in France. Inflation in Germany goes from zero to -12 percent, as does inflation in France.

Step three refers to the policy response. According to the Nash equilibrium there is an increase in European money supply of 12 units, an increase in German government purchases of zero units, and an increase in French government purchases of equally zero units. Step four refers to the outside lag. Unemployment in Germany goes from 12 to zero percent, as does unemployment in France. Inflation in Germany goes from -12 to zero percent, as does inflation in France. The structural deficit in Germany stays at zero percent, as does the structural deficit in France. For a synopsis see Table 4.7.

As a result, given a common demand shock in Europe, monetary and fiscal interaction can achieve zero inflation, zero unemployment, and a zero structural deficit in each of the member countries.

4) A common supply shock in Europe. In each of the member countries let initial unemployment be zero, let initial inflation be zero, and let the initial structural deficit be zero as well. Step one refers to the common supply shock in Europe. In terms of the model there is an increase in B_1 of 12 units, an increase in B_2 of 12 units, an increase in A_1 of 12 units, and an increase in A_2 of equally 12 units. Step two refers to the outside lag. Inflation in Germany goes from zero

to 12 percent, as does inflation in France. Unemployment in Germany goes from zero to 12 percent, as does unemployment in France.

Step three refers to the policy response. According to the Nash equilibrium there is a reduction in European money supply of 12 units, an increase in German government purchases of 12 units, and an increase in French government purchases of equally 12 units. Step four refers to the outside lag. Inflation in Germany stays at 12 percent, as does inflation in France. Unemployment in Germany stays at 12 percent, as does unemployment in France. The structural deficit in Germany goes from zero to 12 percent, as does the structural deficit in France. For an overview see Table 4.11.

Table 4.11
Interaction between European Central Bank,
German Government, and French Government
A Common Supply Shock in Europe

Germany		France	
Unemployment	0	Unemployment	0
Inflation	0	Inflation	0
Structural Deficit	0	Structural Deficit	0
Shock in A_1	12	Shock in A_2	12
Shock in B_1	12	Shock in B_2	12
Unemployment	12	Unemployment	12
Inflation	12	Inflation	12
Δ European Money Supply $-$ 12			
Δ Government Purchases	12	Δ Government Purchases	12
Unemployment	12	Unemployment	12
Inflation	12	Inflation	12
Structural Deficit	12	Structural Deficit	12

As a result, given a common supply shock in Europe, monetary and fiscal interaction has no effect on inflation and unemployment. And what is more, it causes an increase in the structural deficit.

The common supply shock in Europe causes a loss to the European central bank of 576 units, a loss to the German government of 144 units, and a loss to the French government of equally 144 units. However, policy interaction does not reduce the loss of the European central bank. And what is more, it increases the loss of the German government from 144 to 288 units. Correspondingly, it increases the loss of the French government from 144 to 288 units. To sum up, policy interaction increases the loss from 864 to 1152.

5) Summary. Given a demand shock in Germany, policy interaction can achieve zero inflation, zero unemployment, and a zero structural deficit in Europe as a whole. However, it cannot do so in Germany and France. Given a supply shock in Germany, policy interaction has no effect on inflation and unemployment in Europe as a whole. And what is more, it causes an increase in the structural deficit there. Given a common demand shock in Europe, policy interaction can achieve zero inflation, zero unemployment, and a zero structural deficit in each of the member countries. Given a common supply shock in Europe, policy interaction has no effect on inflation and unemployment. And what is more, it causes an increase in the structural deficit.

Chapter 5
Interaction between European Central Bank, German Government, and French Government C

1. The Model

This chapter deals with case C. The targets of the European central bank are zero inflation and zero unemployment in each of the member countries. The targets of the German government are zero unemployment, zero inflation, and a zero structural deficit, in Germany respectively. And the targets of the French government are zero unemployment, zero inflation, and a zero structural deficit, in France respectively.

The model of unemployment, inflation, and the structural deficit can be represented by a system of six equations:

$$u_1 = A_1 - M - G_1 \tag{1}$$

$$u_2 = A_2 - M - G_2 \tag{2}$$

$$\pi_1 = B_1 + M + G_1 \tag{3}$$

$$\pi_2 = B_2 + M + G_2 \tag{4}$$

$$s_1 = G_1 - T_1 \tag{5}$$

$$s_2 = G_2 - T_2 \tag{6}$$

The targets of the European central bank are zero inflation and zero unemployment in each of the member countries. The instrument of the European central bank is European money supply. There are four targets but only one instrument, so what is needed is a loss function. We assume that the European central bank has a quadratic loss function:

$$L = \pi_1^2 + \pi_2^2 + u_1^2 + u_2^2 \tag{7}$$

L is the loss to the European central bank caused by inflation and unemployment in each of the member countries. We assume equal weights in the loss function. The specific target of the European central bank is to minimize the loss, given the inflation functions and the unemployment functions. Taking account of equations (1) to (4), the loss function of the European central bank can be written as follows:

$$L = (B_1 + M + G_1)^2 + (B_2 + M + G_2)^2 \\ + (A_1 - M - G_1)^2 + (A_2 - M - G_2)^2 \tag{8}$$

Then the first-order condition for a minimum loss gives the reaction function of the European central bank:

$$4M = A_1 + A_2 - B_1 - B_2 - 2G_1 - 2G_2 \tag{9}$$

Suppose the German government raises German government purchases. Then, as a response, the European central bank lowers European money supply.

The targets of the German government are zero unemployment, zero inflation, and a zero structural deficit in Germany. The instrument of the German government is German government purchases. There are three targets but only one instrument, so what is needed is a loss function. We assume that the German government has a quadratic loss function:

$$L_1 = \pi_1^2 + u_1^2 + s_1^2 \tag{10}$$

L_1 is the loss to the German government caused by inflation, unemployment, and the structural deficit. We assume equal weights in the loss function. The specific target of the German government is to minimize the loss, given the inflation function, the unemployment function, and the structural deficit function. Taking account of equations (1), (3) and (5), the loss function of the German government can be written as follows:

$$L_1 = (B_1 + M + G_1)^2 + (A_1 - M - G_1)^2 + (G_1 - T_1)^2 \tag{11}$$

Then the first-order condition for a minimum loss gives the reaction function of the German government:

$$3G_1 = A_1 + T_1 - B_1 - 2M \tag{12}$$

Suppose the European central bank lowers European money supply. Then, as a response, the German government raises German government purchases.

The targets of the French government are zero unemployment, zero inflation, and a zero structural deficit in France. The instrument of the French government is French government purchases. There are three targets but only one instrument, so what is needed is a loss function. We assume that the French government has a quadratic loss function:

$$L_2 = \pi_2^2 + u_2^2 + s_2^2 \tag{13}$$

L_2 is the loss to the French government caused by inflation, unemployment, and the structural deficit. We assume equal weights in the loss function. The specific target of the French government is to minimize the loss, given the inflation function, the unemployment function, and the structural deficit function. Taking account of equations (2), (4) and (6), the loss function of the French government can be written as follows:

$$L_2 = (B_2 + M + G_2)^2 + (A_2 - M - G_2)^2 + (G_2 - T_2)^2 \tag{14}$$

Then the first-order condition for a minimum loss gives the reaction function of the French government:

$$3G_2 = A_2 + T_2 - B_2 - 2M \tag{15}$$

Suppose the European central bank lowers European money supply. Then, as a response, the French government raises French government purchases.

The Nash equilibrium is determined by the reaction functions of the European central bank, the German government, and the French government. We assume $T = T_1 = T_2$. The solution to this problem is as follows:

$$4M = A_1 + A_2 - B_1 - B_2 - 4T \tag{16}$$

$$6G_1 = 6T + A_1 - A_2 - B_1 + B_2 \tag{17}$$

$$6G_2 = 6T - A_1 + A_2 + B_1 - B_2 \tag{18}$$

Equations (16), (17) and (18) show the Nash equilibrium of European money supply, German government purchases, and French government purchases. As a result, there is a unique Nash equilibrium. According to equations (16), (17) and (18), an increase in A_1 causes an increase in European money supply, an increase in German government purchases, and a reduction in French government purchases. And an increase in B_1 causes a reduction in European money supply, a reduction in German government purchases, and an increase in French government purchases.

From equations (1), (16) and (17) follows the equilibrium rate of unemployment in Germany:

$$12u_1 = 5B_1 + B_2 + 7A_1 - A_2 \tag{19}$$

And from equations (2), (16) and (18) follows the equilibrium rate of unemployment in France:

$$12u_2 = B_1 + 5B_2 - A_1 + 7A_2 \tag{20}$$

By definition, the rate of unemployment in Europe is:

$$u = 0.5u_1 + 0.5u_2 \tag{21}$$

Making use of equations (19) and (20), the equilibrium rate of unemployment in Europe is:

$$4u = A_1 + A_2 + B_1 + B_2 \tag{22}$$

From equations (3), (16) and (17) follows the equilibrium rate of inflation in Germany:

$$12\pi_1 = 5A_1 + A_2 + 7B_1 - B_2 \tag{23}$$

And from equations (4), (16) and (18) follows the equilibrium rate of inflation in France:

$$12\pi_2 = A_1 + 5A_2 - B_1 + 7B_2 \tag{24}$$

By definition, the rate of inflation in Europe is:

$$\pi = 0.5\pi_1 + 0.5\pi_2 \tag{25}$$

Making use of equations (23) and (24), the equilibrium rate of inflation in Europe is:

$$4\pi = A_1 + A_2 + B_1 + B_2 \tag{26}$$

From equations (5) and (17) follows the equilibrium structural deficit ratio in Germany:

$$6s_1 = A_1 - A_2 - B_1 + B_2 \tag{27}$$

And from equations (6) and (18) follows the equilibrium structural deficit ratio in France:

$$6s_2 = B_1 - B_2 - A_1 + A_2 \tag{28}$$

By definition, the structural deficit ratio in Europe is:

$$s = 0.5s_1 + 0.5s_2 \tag{29}$$

Making use of equations (27) and (28), the equilibrium structural deficit ratio in Europe is:

$$s = 0 \tag{30}$$

The structural deficit in Europe is zero. However, the structural deficits in Germany and France are not zero. What is more, unemployment in Germany,

France and Europe is not zero. And the same applies to inflation in Germany, France and Europe.

2. Some Numerical Examples

For easy reference, the basic model is summarized here:

$$u_1 = A_1 - M - G_1 \tag{1}$$
$$u_2 = A_2 - M - G_2 \tag{2}$$
$$\pi_1 = B_1 + M + G_1 \tag{3}$$
$$\pi_2 = B_2 + M + G_2 \tag{4}$$
$$s_1 = G_1 - T_1 \tag{5}$$
$$s_2 = G_2 - T_2 \tag{6}$$

And the Nash equilibrium can be described by three equations:

$$4M = A_1 + A_2 - B_1 - B_2 - 4T \tag{7}$$
$$6G_1 = 6T + A_1 - A_2 - B_1 + B_2 \tag{8}$$
$$6G_2 = 6T - A_1 + A_2 + B_1 - B_2 \tag{9}$$

It proves useful to study four distinct cases:
- a demand shock in Germany
- a supply shock in Germany
- a common demand shock in Europe
- a common supply shock in Europe.

1) A demand shock in Germany. In each of the member countries let initial unemployment be zero, let initial inflation be zero, and let the initial structural

deficit be zero as well. Step one refers to a decline in the demand for German goods. In terms of the model there is an increase in A_1 of 12 units and a decline in B_1 of equally 12 units. Step two refers to the outside lag. Unemployment in Germany goes from zero to 12 percent. Unemployment in France stays at zero percent. Inflation in Germany goes from zero to -12 percent. Inflation in France stays at zero percent. The structural deficit in Germany stays at zero percent, as does the structural deficit in France.

Step three refers to the policy response. According to the Nash equilibrium there is an increase in European money supply of 6 units, an increase in German government purchases of 4 units, and a reduction in French government purchases of equally 4 units. Step four refers to the outside lag. Unemployment in Germany goes from 12 to 2 percent. Unemployment in France goes from zero to -2 percent. Thus unemployment in Europe goes from 6 to zero percent. Inflation in Germany goes from -12 to -2 percent. Inflation in France goes from zero to 2 percent. Thus inflation in Europe goes from -6 to zero percent. The structural deficit in Germany goes from zero to 4 percent. The structural deficit in France goes from zero to -4 percent. Thus the structural deficit in Europe stays at zero percent. Table 4.12 presents a synopsis.

As a result, given a demand shock in Germany, monetary and fiscal interaction can achieve zero inflation, zero unemployment, and a zero structural deficit in Europe as a whole. However, it cannot do so in Germany and France.

The loss functions of the European central bank, the German government, and the French government are respectively:

$$L = \pi_1^2 + \pi_2^2 + u_1^2 + u_2^2 \tag{10}$$

$$L_1 = \pi_1^2 + u_1^2 + s_1^2 \tag{11}$$

$$L_2 = \pi_2^2 + u_2^2 + s_2^2 \tag{12}$$

The initial loss of the European central bank, the German government, and the French government is zero each. The demand shock in Germany causes a loss to the European central bank of 288 units, a loss to the German government of 288 units, and a loss to the French government of zero units. Then policy interaction reduces the loss of the European central bank from 288 to 16 units. And what is more, it reduces the loss of the German government from 288 to 24 units. On the other hand, it increases the loss of the French government from zero to 24 units.

Table 4.12
Interaction between European Central Bank,
German Government, and French Government
A Demand Shock in Germany

Germany		France	
Unemployment	0	Unemployment	0
Inflation	0	Inflation	0
Structural Deficit	0	Structural Deficit	0
Shock in A_1	12		
Shock in B_1	− 12		
Unemployment	12	Unemployment	0
Inflation	− 12	Inflation	0
Δ European Money Supply	6		
Δ Government Purchases	4	Δ Government Purchases	− 4
Unemployment	2	Unemployment	− 2
Inflation	− 2	Inflation	2
Structural Deficit	4	Structural Deficit	− 4

2) A supply shock in Germany. In each of the member countries let initial unemployment be zero, let initial inflation be zero, and let the initial structural deficit be zero as well. Step one refers to the supply shock in Germany. In terms of the model there is an increase in B_1 of 12 units and an increase in A_1 of equally 12 units. Step two refers to the outside lag. Inflation in Germany goes from zero to 12 percent. Inflation in France stays at zero percent. Unemployment in Germany goes from zero to 12 percent. And unemployment in France stays at zero percent.

Step three refers to the policy response. According to the Nash equilibrium there is no change in European money supply, no change in German government purchases, and no change in French government purchases. Step four refers to the outside lag. Inflation in Germany stays at 12 percent, and inflation in France stays at zero percent. Thus inflation in Europe stays at 6 percent. Unemployment in Germany stays at 12 percent, and unemployment in France stays at zero percent. Thus unemployment in Europe stays at 6 percent. The structural deficit in Germany stays at zero percent, as does the structural deficit in France. Table 4.13 gives an overview.

Table 4.13
Interaction between European Central Bank,
German Government, and French Government
A Supply Shock in Germany

Germany		France	
Unemployment	0	Unemployment	0
Inflation	0	Inflation	0
Structural Deficit	0	Structural Deficit	0
Shock in A_1	12		
Shock in B_1	12		
Unemployment	12	Unemployment	0
Inflation	12	Inflation	0
Δ European Money Supply	0		
Δ Government Purchases	0	Δ Government Purchases	0
Unemployment	12	Unemployment	0
Inflation	12	Inflation	0
Structural Deficit	0	Structural Deficit	0

As a result, given a supply shock in Germany, monetary and fiscal interaction is ineffective. The supply shock in Germany causes a loss to the European central bank of 288 units, a loss to the German government of 288 units, and a loss to the French government of zero units. However, policy interaction cannot reduce the loss of the European central bank, the German government, and the French government.

3) A common demand shock in Europe. In each of the member countries let initial unemployment be zero, let initial inflation be zero, and let the initial structural deficit be zero as well. Step one refers to a decline in the common demand for European goods. In terms of the model there is an increase in A_1 of 12 units, an increase in A_2 of 12 units, a decline in B_1 of 12 units, and a decline in B_2 of equally 12 units. Step two refers to the outside lag. Unemployment in Germany goes from zero to 12 percent, as does unemployment in France. Inflation in Germany goes from zero to -12 percent, as does inflation in France.

Step three refers to the policy response. According to the Nash equilibrium there is an increase in European money supply of 12 units, an increase in German government purchases of zero units, and an increase in French government purchases of equally zero units. Step four refers to the outside lag. Unemployment in Germany goes from 12 to zero percent, as does unemployment in France. Inflation in Germany goes from -12 to zero percent, as does inflation in France. The structural deficit in Germany stays at zero percent, as does the structural deficit in France. For a synopsis see Table 4.7.

As a result, given a common demand shock in Europe, monetary and fiscal interaction can achieve zero inflation, zero unemployment, and a zero structural deficit in each of the member countries.

4) A common supply shock in Europe. In each of the member countries let initial unemployment be zero, let initial inflation be zero, and let the initial structural deficit be zero as well. Step one refers to the common supply shock in Europe. In terms of the model there is an increase in B_1 of 12 units, an increase in B_2 of 12 units, an increase in A_1 of 12 units, and an increase in A_2 of equally 12 units. Step two refers to the outside lag. Inflation in Germany goes from zero to 12 percent, as does inflation in France. Unemployment in Germany goes from zero to 12 percent, as does unemployment in France.

Step three refers to the policy response. According to the Nash equilibrium there is no change in European money supply, no change in German government purchases, and no change in French government purchases. Step four refers to the outside lag. Inflation in Germany stays at 12 percent, as does inflation in France. Unemployment in Germany stays at 12 percent, as does unemployment in France. The structural deficit in Germany stays at zero percent, as does the structural deficit in France. For an overview see Table 4.14. As a result, given a common supply shock in Europe, monetary and fiscal interaction is ineffective.

Table 4.14
Interaction between European Central Bank,
German Government, and French Government
A Common Supply Shock in Europe

Germany		France	
Unemployment	0	Unemployment	0
Inflation	0	Inflation	0
Structural Deficit	0	Structural Deficit	0
Shock in A_1	12	Shock in A_2	12
Shock in B_1	12	Shock in B_2	12
Unemployment	12	Unemployment	12
Inflation	12	Inflation	12
Δ European Money Supply	0		
Δ Government Purchases	0	Δ Government Purchases	0
Unemployment	12	Unemployment	12
Inflation	12	Inflation	12
Structural Deficit	0	Structural Deficit	0

5) Summary. Given a demand shock in Germany, policy interaction can achieve zero inflation, zero unemployment, and a zero structural deficit in Europe as a whole. However, it cannot do so in Germany and France. Given a supply shock in Germany, policy interaction is ineffective. Given a common demand shock in Europe, policy interaction can achieve zero inflation, zero unemployment, and a zero structural deficit in each of the member countries. Given a common supply shock in Europe, policy interaction is ineffective.

6) Comparing cases A, B and C. As to the policy targets there are three distinct cases. In case A the target of the central bank is zero inflation. And the targets of the government are zero unemployment and a zero structural deficit. In case B the targets of the central bank are zero inflation and zero unemployment. And the targets of the government still are zero unemployment and a zero structural deficit. In case C the targets of the central bank are zero inflation and zero unemployment. And the targets of the government are zero unemployment, zero inflation, and a zero structural deficit.

First consider a demand shock in Germany. In case A, given a demand shock in Germany, policy interaction can achieve zero inflation, zero unemployment, and a zero structural deficit in Europe as a whole. However, it cannot do so in Germany and France. In case B, given a demand shock in Germany, policy interaction has the same effects as in case A. And the same holds for case C.

Second consider a supply shock in Germany. In case A, given a supply shock in Germany, policy interaction can achieve zero inflation in Europe as a whole. On the other hand, it causes an increase in both unemployment and the structural deficit. In case B, given a supply shock in Germany, policy interaction has no effect on inflation and unemployment in Europe as a whole. And what is more, it causes an increase in the structural deficit there. In case C, given a supply shock in Germany, policy interaction is ineffective.

Chapter 6
Cooperation between European Central Bank, German Government, and French Government

1. The Model

The model of unemployment, inflation, and the structural deficit can be characterized by a system of six equations:

$$u_1 = A_1 - M - G_1 \tag{1}$$

$$u_2 = A_2 - M - G_2 \tag{2}$$

$$\pi_1 = B_1 + M + G_1 \tag{3}$$

$$\pi_2 = B_2 + M + G_2 \tag{4}$$

$$s_1 = G_1 - T_1 \tag{5}$$

$$s_2 = G_2 - T_2 \tag{6}$$

The policy makers are the European central bank, the German government, and the French government. The targets of policy cooperation are zero inflation, zero unemployment, and a zero structural deficit in each of the member countries. The instruments of policy cooperation are European money supply, German government purchases, and French government purchases. There are six targets but only three instruments, so what is needed is a loss function. We assume that the policy makers agree on a common loss function:

$$L = \pi_1^2 + \pi_2^2 + u_1^2 + u_2^2 + s_1^2 + s_2^2 \tag{7}$$

L is the loss caused by inflation, unemployment, and the structural deficit in each of the member countries. We assume equal weights in the loss function. The specific target of policy cooperation is to minimize the loss, given the inflation functions, the unemployment functions, and the structural deficit functions. Taking account of equations (1) to (6), the loss function under policy cooperation can be written as follows:

$$L = (B_1 + M + G_1)^2 + (B_2 + M + G_2)^2$$
$$+ (A_1 - M - G_1)^2 + (A_2 - M - G_2)^2 \qquad (8)$$
$$+ (G_1 - T_1)^2 + (G_2 - T_2)^2$$

Then the first-order conditions for a minimum loss are:

$$4M = A_1 + A_2 - B_1 - B_2 - 2G_1 - 2G_2 \qquad (9)$$
$$3G_1 = A_1 + T_1 - B_1 - 2M \qquad (10)$$
$$3G_2 = A_2 + T_2 - B_2 - 2M \qquad (11)$$

Equation (9) shows the first-order condition with respect to European money supply. Equation (10) shows the first-order condition with respect to German government purchases. And equation (11) shows the first-order condition with respect to French government purchases.

The cooperative equilibrium is determined by the first-order conditions for a minimum loss. We assume $T = T_1 = T_2$. The solution to this problem is as follows:

$$4M = A_1 + A_2 - B_1 - B_2 - 4T \qquad (12)$$
$$6G_1 = 6T + A_1 - A_2 - B_1 + B_2 \qquad (13)$$
$$6G_2 = 6T - A_1 + A_2 + B_1 - B_2 \qquad (14)$$

Equations (12), (13) and (14) show the cooperative equilibrium of European money supply, German government purchases, and French government purchases. As a result, there is a unique cooperative equilibrium. According to equations (12), (13) and (14), an increase in A_1 causes an increase in European money supply, an increase in German government purchases, and a reduction in French government purchases. And an increase in B_1 causes a reduction in European money supply, a reduction in German government purchases, and an increase in French government purchases.

From equations (1), (12) and (13) follows the optimum rate of unemployment in Germany:

$$12u_1 = 5B_1 + B_2 + 7A_1 - A_2 \tag{15}$$

And from equations (2), (12) and (14) follows the optimum rate of unemployment in France:

$$12u_2 = B_1 + 5B_2 - A_1 + 7A_2 \tag{16}$$

By definition, the rate of unemployment in Europe is:

$$u = 0.5u_1 + 0.5u_2 \tag{17}$$

Making use of equations (15) and (16), the optimum rate of unemployment in Europe is:

$$4u = A_1 + A_2 + B_1 + B_2 \tag{18}$$

From equations (3), (12) and (13) follows the optimum rate of inflation in Germany:

$$12\pi_1 = 5A_1 + A_2 + 7B_1 - B_2 \tag{19}$$

And from equations (4), (12) and (14) follows the optimum rate of inflation in France:

$$12\pi_2 = A_1 + 5A_2 - B_1 + 7B_2 \tag{20}$$

By definition, the rate of inflation in Europe is:

$$\pi = 0.5\pi_1 + 0.5\pi_2 \tag{21}$$

Making use of equations (19) and (20), the optimum rate of inflation in Europe is:

$$4\pi = A_1 + A_2 + B_1 + B_2 \tag{22}$$

From equations (5) and (13) follows the optimum structural deficit ratio in Germany:

$$6s_1 = A_1 - A_2 - B_1 + B_2 \tag{23}$$

And from equations (6) and (14) follows the optimum structural deficit ratio in France:

$$6s_2 = B_1 - B_2 - A_1 + A_2 \tag{24}$$

By definition, the structural deficit ratio in Europe is:

$$s = 0.5s_1 + 0.5s_2 \tag{25}$$

Making use of equations (23) and (24), the optimum structural deficit ratio in Europe is:

$$s = 0 \tag{26}$$

The structural deficit in Europe is zero. However, the structural deficits in Germany and France are not zero. What is more, unemployment in Germany, France and Europe is not zero. And the same applies to inflation in Germany, France and Europe.

2. Some Numerical Examples

For easy reference, the basic model is reproduced here:

$$u_1 = A_1 - M - G_1 \tag{1}$$

$$u_2 = A_2 - M - G_2 \tag{2}$$

$$\pi_1 = B_1 + M + G_1 \tag{3}$$

$$\pi_2 = B_2 + M + G_2 \tag{4}$$

$$s_1 = G_1 - T_1 \tag{5}$$

$$s_2 = G_2 - T_2 \tag{6}$$

And the cooperative equilibrium can be described by three equations:

$$4M = A_1 + A_2 - B_1 - B_2 - 4T \tag{7}$$

$$6G_1 = 6T + A_1 - A_2 - B_1 + B_2 \tag{8}$$

$$6G_2 = 6T - A_1 + A_2 + B_1 - B_2 \tag{9}$$

It proves useful to study four distinct cases:
- a demand shock in Germany
- a supply shock in Germany
- a common demand shock in Europe
- a common supply shock in Europe.

1) A demand shock in Germany. In each of the member countries let initial unemployment be zero, let initial inflation be zero, and let the initial structural deficit be zero as well. Step one refers to a decline in the demand for German goods. In terms of the model there is an increase in A_1 of 12 units and a decline in B_1 of equally 12 units. Step two refers to the outside lag. Unemployment in Germany goes from zero to 12 percent. Unemployment in France stays at zero percent. Inflation in Germany goes from zero to $-$ 12 percent. Inflation in France

stays at zero percent. The structural deficit in Germany stays at zero percent, as does the structural deficit in France.

Step three refers to the policy response. What is needed, according to the model, is an increase in European money supply of 6 units, an increase in German government purchases of 4 units, and a reduction in French government purchases of equally 4 units. Step four refers to the outside lag. Unemployment in Germany goes from 12 to 2 percent. Unemployment in France goes from zero to − 2 percent. Thus unemployment in Europe goes from 6 to zero percent. Inflation in Germany goes from − 12 to − 2 percent. Inflation in France goes from zero to 2 percent. Thus inflation in Europe goes from − 6 to zero percent. The structural deficit in Germany goes from zero to 4 percent. The structural deficit in France goes from zero to − 4 percent. Thus the structural deficit in Europe stays at zero percent. Table 4.15 presents a synopsis.

As a result, given a demand shock in Germany, monetary and fiscal cooperation can achieve zero inflation, zero unemployment, and a zero structural deficit in Europe as a whole. However, it cannot do so in Germany and France. The loss function under policy cooperation is:

$$L = \pi_1^2 + \pi_2^2 + u_1^2 + u_2^2 + s_1^2 + s_2^2 \tag{10}$$

The initial loss is zero. The demand shock in Germany causes a loss of 288 units. Then policy cooperation can reduce the loss to 48 units.

Table 4.15
Cooperation between European Central Bank, German Government, and French Government
A Demand Shock in Germany

Germany		France	
Unemployment	0	Unemployment	0
Inflation	0	Inflation	0
Structural Deficit	0	Structural Deficit	0
Shock in A_1	12		
Shock in B_1	− 12		
Unemployment	12	Unemployment	0
Inflation	− 12	Inflation	0
Δ European Money Supply	6		
Δ Government Purchases	4	Δ Government Purchases	− 4
Unemployment	2	Unemployment	− 2
Inflation	− 2	Inflation	2
Structural Deficit	4	Structural Deficit	− 4

2) A supply shock in Germany. In each of the member countries let initial unemployment be zero, let initial inflation be zero, and let the initial structural deficit be zero as well. Step one refers to the supply shock in Germany. In terms of the model there is an increase in B_1 of 12 units and an increase in A_1 of equally 12 units. Step two refers to the outside lag. Inflation in Germany goes from zero to 12 percent. Inflation in France stays at zero percent. Unemployment in Germany goes from zero to 12 percent. And unemployment in France stays at zero percent.

Step three refers to the policy response. What is needed, according to the model, is to hold European money supply, German government purchases, and French government purchases constant. Step four refers to the outside lag.

Inflation in Germany stays at 12 percent, and inflation in France stays at zero percent. Thus inflation in Europe stays at 6 percent. Unemployment in Germany stays at 12 percent, and unemployment in France stays at zero percent. Thus unemployment in Europe stays at 6 percent. The structural deficit in Germany stays at zero percent, as does the structural deficit in France. Table 4.16 gives an overview.

As a result, given a supply shock in Germany, monetary and fiscal cooperation is ineffective. The supply shock in Germany causes a loss of 288 units. However, policy cooperation cannot reduce the loss.

Table 4.16
Cooperation between European Central Bank,
German Government, and French Government
A Supply Shock in Germany

Germany		France	
Unemployment	0	Unemployment	0
Inflation	0	Inflation	0
Structural Deficit	0	Structural Deficit	0
Shock in A_1	12		
Shock in B_1	12		
Unemployment	12	Unemployment	0
Inflation	12	Inflation	0
Δ European Money Supply	0		
Δ Government Purchases	0	Δ Government Purchases	0
Unemployment	12	Unemployment	0
Inflation	12	Inflation	0
Structural Deficit	0	Structural Deficit	0

3) A common demand shock in Europe. In each of the member countries let initial unemployment be zero, let initial inflation be zero, and let the initial structural deficit be zero as well. Step one refers to a decline in the common demand for European goods. In terms of the model there is an increase in A_1 of 12 units, an increase in A_2 of 12 units, a decline in B_1 of 12 units, and a decline in B_2 of equally 12 units. Step two refers to the outside lag. Unemployment in Germany goes from zero to 12 percent, as does unemployment in France. Inflation in Germany goes from zero to $-$ 12 percent, as does inflation in France.

Step three refers to the policy response. What is needed, according to the model, is an increase in European money supply of 12 units, an increase in German government purchases of zero units, and an increase in French government purchases of equally zero units. Step four refers to the outside lag. Unemployment in Germany goes from 12 to zero percent, as does unemployment in France. Inflation in Germany goes from $-$ 12 to zero percent, as does inflation in France. The structural deficit in Germany stays at zero percent, as does the structural deficit in France. For a synopsis see Table 4.7.

As a result, given a common demand shock in Europe, monetary and fiscal cooperation can achieve zero inflation, zero unemployment, and a zero structural deficit in each of the member countries.

4) A common supply shock in Europe. In each of the member countries let initial unemployment be zero, let initial inflation be zero, and let the initial structural deficit be zero as well. Step one refers to the common supply shock in Europe. In terms of the model there is an increase in B_1 of 12 units, an increase in B_2 of 12 units, an increase in A_1 of 12 units, and an increase in A_2 of equally 12 units. Step two refers to the outside lag. Inflation in Germany goes from zero to 12 percent, as does inflation in France. Unemployment in Germany goes from zero to 12 percent, as does unemployment in France.

Step three refers to the policy response. What is needed, according to the model, is to hold European money supply, German government purchases, and French government purchases constant. Step four refers to the outside lag. Inflation in Germany stays at 12 percent, as does inflation in France. Unemployment in Germany stays at 12 percent, as does unemployment in France. The structural deficit in Germany stays at zero percent, as does the structural deficit in France. For an overview see Table 4.14. As a result, given a common supply shock in Europe, monetary and fiscal cooperation is ineffective.

5) Summary. Given a demand shock in Germany, policy cooperation can achieve zero inflation, zero unemployment, and a zero structural deficit in Europe as a whole. However, it cannot do so in Germany and France. Given a supply shock in Germany, policy cooperation is ineffective. Given a common demand shock in Europe, policy cooperation can achieve zero inflation, zero unemployment, and a zero structural deficit in each of the member countries. Given a common supply shock in Europe, policy cooperation is ineffective.

6) Comparing policy cooperation with policy interaction. First consider the targets of policy interaction. By assumption, the targets of the European central bank are zero inflation in Germany and France. The targets of the German government are zero unemployment and a zero structural deficit in Germany. And the targets of the French government are zero unemployment and a zero structural deficit in France. There are equal weights in each of the loss functions. Second consider the targets of policy cooperation. By assumption, the targets are zero inflation, zero unemployment, and a zero structural deficit in each of the member countries. There are equal weights in the common loss function.

Now consider a demand shock in Germany. Given a demand shock in Germany, policy interaction can achieve zero inflation, zero unemployment, and a zero structural deficit in Europe as a whole. However, it cannot do so in Germany and France. Given a demand shock in Germany, policy cooperation has the same effects as policy interaction. Then consider a supply shock in Germany. Given a supply shock in Germany, policy interaction can achieve zero inflation in Europe as a whole. On the other hand, it causes an increase in both unemployment and the structural deficit. By contrast, given a supply shock in Germany, policy cooperation is ineffective.

Synopsis

Table 5.1
The Monetary Union as a Whole
Absence of a Deficit Target

Interaction between European Central Bank and European Government	No Unique Nash Equilibrium
Cooperation between European Central Bank and European Government	Multiple Solutions

Table 5.2
The Monetary Union as a Whole
Presence of a Deficit Target

Interaction between European Central Bank and European Government	Unique Nash Equilibrium
Cooperation between European Central Bank and European Government	Unique Solution
Generally, Cooperative Solution Is Different from Nash Equilibrium	

Table 5.3
The Monetary Union of Two Countries
Absence of a Deficit Target

Interaction between European Central Bank, German Government, and French Government	No Unique Nash Equilibrium
Cooperation between European Central Bank, German Government, and French Government	Multiple Solutions

Table 5.4
The Monetary Union of Two Countries
Presence of a Deficit Target

Interaction between European Central Bank, German Government, and French Government	Unique Nash Equilibrium
Cooperation between European Central Bank, German Government, and French Government	Unique Solution
Generally, Cooperative Solution Is Different from Nash Equilibrium	

Conclusion

1. The Monetary Union as a Whole: Absence of a Deficit Target

1.1. Interaction between Central Bank and Government

An increase in European money supply lowers unemployment in Europe. On the other hand, it raises inflation there. Correspondingly, an increase in European government purchases lowers unemployment in Europe. On the other hand, it raises inflation there.

In the numerical example, a unit increase in money supply lowers the rate of unemployment by 1 percentage point. On the other hand, it raises the rate of inflation by 1 percentage point. Similarly, a unit increase in government purchases lowers the rate of unemployment by 1 percentage point. On the other hand, it raises the rate of inflation by 1 percentage point. For instance, let initial unemployment be 2 percent, and let initial inflation be 2 percent as well. Now consider a unit increase in money supply. Then unemployment goes from 2 to 1 percent. On the other hand, inflation goes from 2 to 3 percent.

The target of the European central bank is zero inflation in Europe. The instrument of the European central bank is European money supply. Thus there is one target and one instrument. We assume that the European central bank has a quadratic loss function. The amount of loss depends on the level of inflation. The European central bank sets European money supply so as to minimize its loss. The first-order condition for a minimum loss gives the reaction function of the European central bank. Suppose the European government raises European government purchases. Then, as a response, the European central bank lowers European money supply.

The target of the European government is zero unemployment in Europe. The instrument of the European government is European government purchases. Hence there is one target and one instrument. We assume that the European government has a quadratic loss function. The amount of loss depends on the level of unemployment. The European government sets European government purchases so as to minimize its loss. The first-order condition for a minimum loss gives the reaction function of the European government. Suppose the European central bank lowers European money supply. Then, as a response, the European government raises European government purchases.

The Nash equilibrium is determined by the reaction functions of the European central bank and the European government. In principle, it yields the equilibrium levels of European money supply and European government purchases. As a result, two cases can occur. In the first case there is no Nash equilibrium. And in the second case there are multiple Nash equilibria.

1.2. Cooperation between Central Bank and Government

1) The model. The policy makers are the European central bank and the European government. The targets of policy cooperation are zero inflation and zero unemployment in Europe. The instruments of policy cooperation are European money supply and European government purchases. Thus there are two targets and two instruments. We assume that the policy makers agree on a common loss function. The amount of loss depends on inflation and unemployment. The policy makers set European money supply and European government purchases so as to minimize the common loss.

The cooperative equilibrium is determined by the first-order conditions for a minimum loss. It yields the optimum combinations of European money supply and European government purchases. As a result, given a shock, monetary and fiscal cooperation can reduce the existing loss.

2) A numerical example of a demand shock. We assume equal weights in the loss function. Let initial unemployment be 2 percent, and let initial inflation be − 2 percent. Step one refers to the policy response. A first solution is an increase in

money supply of 2 units and an increase in government purchases of zero units. Step two refers to the outside lag. Unemployment goes from 2 to zero percent. And inflation goes from − 2 to zero percent. Table 6.1 presents a synopsis.

As a result, given a demand shock, policy cooperation can achieve both zero inflation and zero unemployment. A second solution is an increase in money supply of 1 unit and an increase in government purchases of equally 1 unit. A third solution is an increase in money supply of zero units and an increase in government purchases of 2 units. And so on.

Table 6.1
Cooperation between Central Bank and Government
A Demand Shock

Unemployment	2	Inflation	− 2
Change in Money Supply	2	Change in Govt Purchases	0
Unemployment	0	Inflation	0

3) A numerical example of a supply shock. Let initial inflation be 2 percent, and let initial unemployment be 2 percent as well. Step one refers to the policy response. A first solution is to keep money supply and government purchases constant. As a result, given a supply shock, policy cooperation is ineffective.

4) A numerical example of a mixed shock. Let initial inflation be 4 percent, and let initial unemployment be zero percent. Step one refers to the policy response. A first solution is a reduction in money supply of 2 units and a reduction in government purchases of zero units. Step two refers to the outside lag. Inflation goes from 4 to 2 percent. And unemployment goes from zero to 2 percent. Table 6.2 gives an overview.

As a result, given a mixed shock, policy cooperation can reduce the loss caused by inflation and unemployment. However, it cannot achieve zero inflation and zero unemployment. A second solution is a reduction in money supply of 1 unit and a reduction in government purchases of equally 1 unit. A third solution is a reduction in money supply of zero units and a reduction in government purchases of 2 units. And so on.

Table 6.2
Cooperation between Central Bank and Government
A Mixed Shock

Unemployment	0	Inflation	4
Change in Money Supply	− 2	Change in Govt Purchases	0
Unemployment	2	Inflation	2

5) Comparing policy cooperation with policy interaction. Under policy interaction there is no unique Nash equilibrium. By contrast, policy cooperation can reduce the loss caused by inflation and unemployment. Judging from this point of view, policy cooperation seems to be superior to policy interaction.

2. The Monetary Union as a Whole: Presence of a Deficit Target

2.1. Interaction between Central Bank and Government

1) The model. An increase in European money supply lowers unemployment in Europe. On the other hand, it raises inflation there. However, it has no effect on the structural deficit. Correspondingly, an increase in European government purchases lowers unemployment in Europe. On the other hand, it raises inflation there. And what is more, it raises the structural deficit.

In the numerical example, a unit increase in money supply lowers the rate of unemployment by 1 percentage point. On the other hand, it raises the rate of inflation by 1 percentage point. However, it has no effect on the structural deficit ratio. Similarly, a unit increase in government purchases lowers the rate of unemployment by 1 percentage point. On the other hand, it raises the rate of inflation by 1 percentage point. And what is more, it raises the structural deficit ratio by 1 percentage point. For instance, let initial unemployment be 2 percent, let initial inflation be 2 percent, and let the initial structural deficit be 2 percent as well. Now consider a unit increase in government purchases. Then unemployment goes from 2 to 1 percent. On the other hand, inflation goes from 2 to 3 percent. And what is more, the structural deficit goes from 2 to 3 percent as well.

The target of the European central bank is zero inflation in Europe. The instrument of the European central bank is European money supply. Thus there is one target and one instrument. We assume that the European central bank has a quadratic loss function. The amount of loss depends on the level of inflation. The European central bank sets European money supply so as to minimize its loss. Then the first-order condition for a minimum loss gives the reaction function of the European central bank.

The targets of the European government are zero unemployment and a zero structural deficit in Europe. The instrument of the European government is

European government purchases. There are two targets but only one instrument, so what is needed is a loss function. We assume that the European government has a quadratic loss function. The amount of loss depends on unemployment and the structural deficit in Europe. The European government sets European government purchases so as to minimize its loss. Then the first-order condition for a minimum loss gives the reaction function of the European government.

The Nash equilibrium is determined by the reaction functions of the European central bank and the European government. It yields the equilibrium levels of European money supply and European government purchases. As a result, given a shock, monetary and fiscal interaction can reduce the existing loss.

2) A numerical example of a demand shock. We assume equal weights in the loss function of the government. Let initial unemployment be 2 percent, let initial inflation be − 2 percent, and let the initial structural deficit be zero percent. Step one refers to the policy response. According to the Nash equilibrium there is an increase in money supply of 2 units and an increase in government purchases of zero units. Step two refers to the outside lag. Unemployment goes from 2 to zero percent. Inflation goes from − 2 to zero percent. And the structural deficit stays at zero percent. Table 6.3 presents a synopsis. As a result, given a demand shock, policy interaction can achieve zero inflation, zero unemployment, and a zero structural deficit.

Table 6.3
Interaction between Central Bank and Government
A Demand Shock

Unemployment	2	Inflation	− 2
Structural Deficit	0		
Change in Money Supply	2	Change in Govt Purchases	0
Unemployment	0	Inflation	0
Structural Deficit	0		

3) A numerical example of a supply shock. Let initial inflation be 2 percent, let initial unemployment be 2 percent as well, and let the initial structural deficit be zero percent. Step one refers to the policy response. According to the Nash equilibrium there is a reduction in money supply of 6 units and an increase in government purchases of 4 units. Step two refers to the outside lag. Inflation goes from 2 to zero percent. Unemployment goes from 2 to 4 percent. And the structural deficit goes from zero to 4 percent. Table 6.4 gives an overview. As a result, given a supply shock, policy interaction can achieve zero inflation. On the other hand, it causes an increase in unemployment and an increase in the structural deficit.

Table 6.4
Interaction between Central Bank and Government
A Supply Shock

Unemployment	2	Inflation	2
Structural Deficit	0		
Change in Money Supply	− 6	Change in Govt Purchases	4
Unemployment	4	Inflation	0
Structural Deficit	4		

2.2. Cooperation between Central Bank and Government

1) The model. The policy makers are the European central bank and the European government. The targets of policy cooperation are zero inflation, zero unemployment, and a zero structural deficit. The instruments of policy cooperation are European money supply and European government purchases. There are three targets but only two instruments, so what is needed is a loss function. We assume that the policy makers agree on a common loss function. The amount of loss depends on inflation, unemployment, and the structural deficit. The policy makers set European money supply and European government purchases so as to minimize the common loss.

The cooperative equilibrium is determined by the first-order conditions for a minimum loss. It yields the optimum levels of European money supply and European government purchases. As a result, given a shock, monetary and fiscal cooperation can reduce the existing loss.

2) A numerical example of a demand shock. We assume equal weights in the loss function. Let initial unemployment be 2 percent, let initial inflation be − 2 percent, and let the initial structural deficit be zero percent. Step one refers to the policy response. What is needed, according to the model, is an increase in money supply of 2 units and an increase in government purchases of zero units. Step two refers to the outside lag. Unemployment goes from 2 to zero percent. Inflation goes from − 2 to zero percent. And the structural deficit stays at zero percent. For a synopsis see Table 6.5. As a result, given a demand shock, policy cooperation can achieve zero inflation, zero unemployment, and a zero structural deficit.

3) A numerical example of a supply shock. Let initial inflation be 2 percent, let initial unemployment be 2 percent as well, and let the initial structural deficit be zero percent. Step one refers to the policy response. What is needed, according to the model, is to keep money supply and government purchases constant. As a result, given a supply shock, policy cooperation is ineffective.

4) Comparing policy cooperation with policy interaction. First consider a demand shock. Given a demand shock, policy interaction can achieve zero

inflation, zero unemployment, and a zero structural deficit. Given a demand shock, policy cooperation has the same effects as policy interaction. Second consider a supply shock. Given a supply shock, policy interaction can achieve zero inflation. On the other hand, it causes an increase in both unemployment and the structural deficit. By contrast, given a supply shock, policy cooperation is ineffective.

Table 6.5
Cooperation between Central Bank and Government
A Demand Shock

Unemployment	2	Inflation	-2
Structural Deficit	0		
Change in Money Supply	2	Change in Govt Purchases	0
Unemployment	0	Inflation	0
Structural Deficit	0		

3. The Monetary Union of Two Countries: Absence of a Deficit Target

3.1. Interaction between European Central Bank, German Government, and French Government

The monetary union consists of two countries, say Germany and France. The member countries are the same size and have the same behavioural functions. An increase in European money supply lowers unemployment in Germany and France. On the other hand, it raises inflation there. An increase in German government purchases lowers unemployment in Germany. On the other hand, it raises inflation there. Correspondingly, an increase in French government purchases lowers unemployment in France. On the other hand, it raises inflation there.

In the numerical example, a unit increase in European money supply lowers the rates of unemployment in Germany and France by 1 percentage point each. On the other hand, it raises the rates of inflation there by 1 percentage point each. A unit increase in German government purchases lowers the rate of unemployment in Germany by 1 percentage point. On the other hand, it raises the rate of inflation there by 1 percentage point. Similarly, a unit increase in French government purchases lowers the rate of unemployment in France by 1 percentage point. On the other hand, it raises the rate of inflation there by 1 percentage point.

For instance, let initial unemployment in Germany be 3 percent, and let initial unemployment in France be 1 percent. Further let initial inflation in Germany be 3 percent, and let initial inflation in France be 1 percent. Now consider a unit increase in European money supply. Then unemployment in Germany goes from 3 to 2 percent, and unemployment in France goes from 1 to zero percent. On the other hand, inflation in Germany goes from 3 to 4 percent, and inflation in France goes from 1 to 2 percent.

The targets of the European central bank are zero inflation in Germany and France. The instrument of the European central bank is European money supply.

There are two targets but only one instrument, so what is needed is a loss function. We assume that the European central bank has a quadratic loss function. The amount of loss depends on inflation in Germany and France. The European central bank sets European money supply so as to minimize its loss. The first-order condition for a minimum loss gives the reaction function of the European central bank. Suppose the German government raises German government purchases. Then, as a response, the European central bank lowers European money supply.

The target of the German government is zero unemployment in Germany. The instrument of the German government is German government purchases. Thus there is one target and one instrument. We assume that the German government has a quadratic loss function. The amount of loss depends on unemployment in Germany. The German government sets German government purchases so as to minimize its loss. The first-order condition for a minimum loss gives the reaction function of the German government. Suppose the European central bank lowers European money supply. Then, as a response, the German government raises German government purchases.

Correspondingly, the target of the French government is zero unemployment in France. The instrument of the French government is French government purchases. Hence there is one target and one instrument. We assume that the French government has a quadratic loss function. The amount of loss depends on unemployment in France. The French government sets French government purchases so as to minimize its loss. The first-order condition for a minimum loss gives the reaction function of the French government. Suppose the European central bank lowers European money supply. Then, as a response, the French government raises French government purchases.

The Nash equilibrium is determined by the reaction functions of the European central bank, the German government, and the French government. In principle, it yields the equilibrium levels of European money supply, German government purchases, and French government purchases. As a result, two cases can occur. In the first case there is no Nash equilibrium. And in the second case there are multiple Nash equilibria.

3.2. Cooperation between European Central Bank, German Government, and French Government

1) The model. The policy makers are the European central bank, the German government, and the French government. The targets of policy cooperation are zero inflation and zero unemployment in each of the member countries. The instruments of policy cooperation are European money supply, German government purchases, and French government purchases. There are four targets but only three instruments, so what is needed is a loss function. We assume that the policy makers agree on a common loss function. The amount of loss depends on inflation and unemployment in each of the member countries. The policy makers set European money supply, German government purchases, and French government purchases so as to minimize the common loss.

The cooperative equilibrium is determined by the first-order conditions for a minimum loss. It yields the optimum combinations of European money supply, German government purchases, and French government purchases. As a result, given a shock, monetary and fiscal cooperation can reduce the existing loss.

2) A numerical example of a demand shock in Germany. We assume equal weights in the loss function. Let initial unemployment in Germany be 2 percent, and let initial unemployment in France be zero percent. Further let initial inflation in Germany be − 2 percent, and let initial inflation in France be zero percent. Step one refers to the policy response. A first solution is an increase in European money supply of 1 unit, an increase in German government purchases of 1 unit, and a reduction in French government purchases of equally 1 unit. Step two refers to the outside lag. Unemployment in Germany goes from 2 to zero percent. Unemployment in France stays at zero percent. Inflation in Germany goes from − 2 to zero percent. And inflation in France stays at zero percent. Table 6.6 presents a synopsis.

As a result, given a demand shock in Germany, policy cooperation can achieve zero inflation and zero unemployment in each of the member countries. A second solution is an increase in European money supply of 2 units, an increase in German government purchases of zero units, and a reduction in

French government purchases of 2 units. A third solution is an increase in European money supply of zero units, an increase in German government purchases of 2 units, and a reduction in French government purchases of zero units. And so on.

Table 6.6
Cooperation between European Central Bank, German Government, and French Government
A Demand Shock in Germany

Germany		France	
Unemployment	2	Unemployment	0
Inflation	−2	Inflation	0
Δ European Money Supply	1		
Δ Government Purchases	1	Δ Government Purchases	−1
Unemployment	0	Unemployment	0
Inflation	0	Inflation	0

3) A numerical example of a supply shock in Germany. Let initial inflation in Germany be 2 percent, and let initial inflation in France be zero percent. Further let initial unemployment in Germany be 2 percent, and let initial unemployment in France be zero percent. Step one refers to the policy response. A first solution is to keep money supply and government purchases constant. As a result, given a supply shock in Germany, policy cooperation is ineffective.

4) A numerical example of a mixed shock in Germany. Let initial inflation in Germany be 4 percent, and let initial inflation in France be zero percent. Further let initial unemployment in Germany and France be zero percent each. Step one refers to the policy response. A first solution is a reduction in European money supply of 1 unit, a reduction in German government purchases of 1 unit, and an increase in French government purchases of equally 1 unit. Step two refers to the

outside lag. Inflation in Germany goes from 4 to 2 percent. Inflation in France stays at zero percent. Unemployment in Germany goes from zero to 2 percent. And unemployment in France stays at zero percent. For a synopsis see Table 6.7.

As a result, given a mixed shock in Germany, policy cooperation can reduce the loss caused by inflation and unemployment. However, it cannot achieve zero inflation and zero unemployment in each of the member countries.

Table 6.7
Cooperation between European Central Bank,
German Government, and French Government
A Mixed Shock in Germany

Germany		France	
Unemployment	0	Unemployment	0
Inflation	4	Inflation	0
Δ European Money Supply	-1		
Δ Government Purchases	-1	Δ Government Purchases	1
Unemployment	2	Unemployment	0
Inflation	2	Inflation	0

5) Comparing policy cooperation with policy interaction. Under policy interaction there is no unique Nash equilibrium. By contrast, policy cooperation can reduce the loss caused by inflation and unemployment. Judging from this point of view, policy cooperation seems to be superior to policy interaction.

4. The Monetary Union of Two Countries: Presence of a Deficit Target

4.1. Interaction between European Central Bank, German Government, and French Government

1) The model. An increase in European money supply lowers unemployment in Germany and France. On the other hand, it raises inflation there. However, it has no effect on structural deficits. An increase in German government purchases lowers unemployment in Germany. On the other hand, it raises inflation there. And what is more, it raises the structural deficit. Correspondingly, an increase in French government purchases lowers unemployment in France. On the other hand, it raises inflation there. And what is more, it raises the structural deficit.

In the numerical example, a unit increase in European money supply lowers the rates of unemployment in Germany and France by 1 percentage point each. On the other hand, it raises the rates of inflation there by 1 percentage point each. However, it has no effect on the structural deficit ratios there. A unit increase in German government purchases lowers the rate of unemployment in Germany by 1 percentage point. On the other hand, it raises the rate of inflation there by 1 percentage point. And what is more, it raises the structural deficit ratio there by 1 percentage point as well. Similarly, a unit increase in French government purchases lowers the rate of unemployment in France by 1 percentage point. On the other hand, it raises the rate of inflation there by 1 percentage point. And what is more, it raises the structural deficit ratio there by 1 percentage point as well.

For instance, let initial unemployment in Germany be 2 percent, let initial inflation in Germany be 2 percent, and let the initial structural deficit in Germany be 2 percent as well. Now consider a unit increase in German government purchases. Then unemployment in Germany goes from 2 to 1 percent. On the other hand, inflation in Germany goes from 2 to 3 percent. And what is more, the structural deficit in Germany goes from 2 to 3 percent as well.

The targets of the European central bank are zero inflation in Germany and France. The instrument of the European central bank is European money supply. There are two targets but only one instrument, so what is needed is a loss function. We assume that the European central bank has a quadratic loss function. The amount of loss depends on inflation in Germany and France. The European central bank sets European money supply so as to minimize its loss. Then the first-order condition for a minimum loss gives the reaction function of the European central bank.

The targets of the German government are zero unemployment and a zero structural deficit in Germany. The instrument of the German government is German government purchases. There are two targets but only one instrument, so what is needed is a loss function. We assume that the German government has a quadratic loss function. The amount of loss depends on unemployment and the structural deficit in Germany. The German government sets German government purchases so as to minimize its loss. Then the first-order condition for a minimum loss gives the reaction function of the German government.

The targets of the French government are zero unemployment and a zero structural deficit in France. The instrument of the French government is French government purchases. There are two targets but only one instrument, so what is needed is a loss function. We assume that the French government has a quadratic loss function. The amount of loss depends on unemployment and the structural deficit in France. The French government sets French government purchases so as to minimize its loss. Then the first-order condition for a minimum loss gives the reaction function of the French government.

The Nash equilibrium is determined by the reaction functions of the European central bank, the German government, and the French government. It yields the equilibrium levels of European money supply, German government purchases, and French government purchases. As a result, given a shock, monetary and fiscal interaction can reduce the existing loss.

2) A numerical example of a demand shock in Germany. We assume equal weights in each of the loss functions. Let initial unemployment in Germany be 12 percent, and let initial unemployment in France zero percent. Let initial inflation in Germany be – 12 percent, and let initial inflation in France be zero percent.

Further let the initial structural deficits in Germany and France be zero percent each. Step one refers to the policy response. According to the Nash equilibrium there is an increase in European money supply of 6 units, an increase in German government purchases of 3 units, and a reduction in French government purchases of equally 3 units.

Step two refers to the outside lag. Unemployment in Germany goes from 12 to 3 percent. Unemployment in France goes from zero to − 3 percent. Thus unemployment in Europe goes from 6 to zero percent. Inflation in Germany goes from − 12 to − 3 percent. Inflation in France goes from zero to 3 percent. Thus inflation in Europe goes from − 6 to zero percent. The structural deficit in Germany goes from zero to 3 percent. The structural deficit in France goes from zero to − 3 percent. Thus the structural deficit in Europe stays at zero percent. Table 6.8 presents a synopsis.

As a result, given a demand shock in Germany, policy interaction can achieve zero inflation, zero unemployment, and a zero structural deficit in Europe as a whole. However, it cannot do so in Germany and France.

Table 6.8
Interaction between European Central Bank,
German Government, and French Government
A Demand Shock in Germany

Germany		France	
Unemployment	12	Unemployment	0
Inflation	− 12	Inflation	0
Δ European Money Supply	6		
Δ Government Purchases	3	Δ Government Purchases	− 3
Unemployment	3	Unemployment	− 3
Inflation	− 3	Inflation	3
Structural Deficit	3	Structural Deficit	− 3

3) A numerical example of a supply shock in Germany. Let initial inflation in Germany be 12 percent, and let initial inflation in France be zero percent. Let initial unemployment in Germany be 12 percent, and let initial unemployment in France be zero percent. Further let the initial structural deficits in Germany and France be zero percent each. Step one refers to the policy response. According to the Nash equilibrium there is a reduction in European money supply of 18 units, an increase in German government purchases of 15 units, and an increase in French government purchases of 9 units.

Step two refers to the outside lag. Inflation in Germany goes from 12 to 9 percent. Inflation in France goes from zero to − 9 percent. Thus inflation in Europe goes from 6 to zero percent. Unemployment in Germany goes from 12 to 15 percent. Unemployment in France goes from zero to 9 percent. Thus unemployment in Europe goes from 6 to 12 percent. The structural deficit in Germany goes from zero to 15 percent. The structural deficit in France goes from zero to 9 percent. Thus the structural deficit in Europe goes from zero to 12 percent. Table 6.9 gives an overview.

As a result, given a supply shock in Germany, policy interaction can achieve zero inflation in Europe as a whole. On the other hand, it causes an increase in both unemployment and the structural deficit.

4) A common demand shock in Europe. As a result, policy interaction can achieve zero inflation, zero unemployment, and a zero structural deficit in each of the member countries.

5) A common supply shock in Europe. As a result, policy interaction can achieve zero inflation in each of the member countries. On the other hand, it causes an increase in both unemployment and the structural deficit there.

Table 6.9
**Interaction between European Central Bank,
German Government, and French Government**
A Supply Shock in Germany

	Germany		France	
Unemployment	12	Unemployment	0
Inflation	12	Inflation	0
Δ European Money Supply − 18			
Δ Government Purchases	15	Δ Government Purchases	9
Unemployment	15	Unemployment	9
Inflation	9	Inflation	− 9
Structural Deficit	15	Structural Deficit	9

4.2. Cooperation between European Central Bank, German Government, and French Government

1) The model. The policy makers are the European central bank, the German government, and the French government. The targets of policy cooperation are zero inflation, zero unemployment, and a zero structural deficit in each of the member countries. The instruments of policy cooperation are European money supply, German government purchases, and French government purchases. There are six targets but only three instruments, so what is needed is a loss function. We assume that the policy makers agree on a common loss function. The amount of loss depends on inflation, unemployment, and the structural deficit in each of the member countries. The policy makers set European money supply, German government purchases, and French government purchases so as to minimize the common loss.

The cooperative equilibrium is determined by the first-order conditions for a minimum loss. It yields the optimum levels of European money supply, German government purchases, and French government purchases. As a result, given a shock, monetary and fiscal cooperation can reduce the existing loss.

2) A numerical example of a demand shock in Germany. We assume equal weights in the loss function. Let initial unemployment in Germany be 12 percent, and let initial unemployment in France be zero percent. Let initial inflation in Germany be − 12 percent, and let initial inflation in France be zero percent. Further let the initial structural deficits in Germany and France be zero percent each. Step one refers to the policy response. What is needed, according to the model, is an increase in European money supply of 6 units, an increase in German government purchases of 4 units, and a reduction in French government purchases of equally 4 units.

Step two refers to the outside lag. Unemployment in Germany goes from 12 to 2 percent. Unemployment in France goes from zero to − 2 percent. Thus unemployment in Europe goes from 6 to zero percent. Inflation in Germany goes from − 12 to − 2 percent. Inflation in France goes from zero to 2 percent. Thus inflation in Europe goes from − 6 to zero percent. The structural deficit in

Germany goes from zero to 4 percent. The structural deficit in France goes from zero to − 4 percent. Thus the structural deficit in Europe stays at zero percent. Table 6.10 presents a synopsis.

As a result, given a demand shock in Germany, policy cooperation can achieve zero inflation, zero unemployment, and a zero structural deficit in Europe as a whole. However, it cannot do so in Germany and France.

Table 6.10
Cooperation between European Central Bank,
German Government, and French Government
A Demand Shock in Germany

Germany		France	
Unemployment	12	Unemployment	0
Inflation	− 12	Inflation	0
Δ European Money Supply	6		
Δ Government Purchases	4	Δ Government Purchases	− 4
Unemployment	2	Unemployment	− 2
Inflation	− 2	Inflation	2
Structural Deficit	4	Structural Deficit	− 4

3) A numerical example of a supply shock in Germany. Let initial inflation in Germany be 12 percent, and let initial inflation in France be zero percent. Let initial unemployment in Germany be 12 percent, and let initial unemployment in France be zero percent. Further let the initial structural deficits in Germany and France be zero percent each. Step one refers to the policy response. What is needed, according to the model, is to hold European money supply, German government purchases, and French government purchases constant. As a result, given a supply shock in Germany, policy cooperation is ineffective.

4) A common demand shock in Europe. As a result, given a common demand shock in Europe, policy cooperation can achieve zero inflation, zero unemployment, and a zero structural deficit in each of the member countries.

5) A common supply shock in Europe. As a result, given a common supply shock in Europe, policy cooperation is ineffective.

6) Comparing policy cooperation with policy interaction. First consider a demand shock in Germany. Given a demand shock in Germany, policy interaction can achieve zero inflation, zero unemployment, and a zero structural deficit in Europe as a whole. However, it cannot do so in Germany and France. Given a demand shock in Germany, policy cooperation has the same effects as policy interaction. Second consider a supply shock in Germany. Given a supply shock in Germany, policy interaction can achieve zero inflation in Europe as a whole. On the other hand, it causes an increase in both unemployment and the structural deficit. By contrast, given a supply shock in Germany, policy cooperation is ineffective.

Result

1. The Monetary Union of Two Countries: Absence of a Deficit Target

1.1. Interaction between European Central Bank, German Government, and French Government

The targets of the European central bank are zero inflation in Germany and France. The instrument of the European central bank is European money supply. We assume that the European central bank has a quadratic loss function. The amount of loss depends on inflation in Germany and France. The European central bank sets European money supply so as to minimize its loss. The first-order condition for a minimum loss gives the reaction function of the European central bank. Suppose the German government raises German government purchases. Then, as a response, the European central bank lowers European money supply.

The target of the German government is zero unemployment in Germany. The instrument of the German government is German government purchases. We assume that the German government has a quadratic loss function. The amount of loss depends on unemployment in Germany. The German government sets German government purchases so as to minimize its loss. The first-order condition for a minimum loss gives the reaction function of the German government. Suppose the European central bank lowers European money supply. Then, as a response, the German government raises German government purchases.

Correspondingly, the target of the French government is zero unemployment in France. The instrument of the French government is French government purchases. We assume that the French government has a quadratic loss function. The amount of loss depends on unemployment in France. The French government sets French government purchases so as to minimize its loss. The first-order condition for a minimum loss gives the reaction function of the French government. Suppose the European central bank lowers European money supply. Then, as a response, the French government raises French government purchases.

The Nash equilibrium is determined by the reaction functions of the European central bank, the German government, and the French government. In principle, it yields the equilibrium levels of European money supply, German government purchases, and French government purchases. As a result, two cases can occur. In the first case there is no Nash equilibrium. And in the second case there are multiple Nash equilibria.

1.2. Cooperation between European Central Bank, German Government, and French Government

The targets of policy cooperation are zero inflation and zero unemployment in each of the member countries. The instruments of policy cooperation are European money supply, German government purchases, and French government purchases. We assume that the policy makers agree on a common loss function. The amount of loss depends on inflation and unemployment in each of the member countries. The policy makers set European money supply, German government purchases, and French government purchases so as to minimize the common loss.

The cooperative equilibrium is determined by the first-order conditions for a minimum loss. It yields the optimum combinations of European money supply, German government purchases, and French government purchases. Given a demand shock in Germany, policy cooperation can achieve zero inflation and zero unemployment in each of the member countries. Given a supply shock in Germany, policy cooperation is ineffective. Given a mixed shock in Germany, policy cooperation can reduce the loss to a certain extent.

2. The Monetary Union of Two Countries: Presence of a Deficit Target

2.1. Interaction between European Central Bank, German Government, and French Government

The targets of the European central bank are zero inflation in Germany and France. The instrument of the European central bank is European money supply. We assume that the European central bank has a quadratic loss function. The amount of loss depends on inflation in Germany and France. The European central bank sets European money supply so as to minimize its loss. Then the first-order condition for a minimum loss gives the reaction function of the European central bank.

The targets of the German government are zero unemployment and a zero structural deficit in Germany. The instrument of the German government is German government purchases. We assume that the German government has a quadratic loss function. The amount of loss depends on unemployment and the structural deficit in Germany. The German government sets German government purchases so as to minimize its loss. Then the first-order condition for a minimum loss gives the reaction function of the German government.

The targets of the French government are zero unemployment and a zero structural deficit in France. The instrument of the French government is French government purchases. We assume that the French government has a quadratic loss function. The amount of loss depends on unemployment and the structural deficit in France. The French government sets French government purchases so as to minimize its loss. Then the first-order condition for a minimum loss gives the reaction function of the French government.

The Nash equilibrium is determined by the reaction functions of the European central bank, the German government, and the French government. It yields the equilibrium levels of European money supply, German government purchases, and French government purchases.

Given a demand shock in Germany, policy interaction can achieve zero inflation, zero unemployment, and a zero structural deficit in Europe as a whole. However, it cannot do so in Germany and France. Given a supply shock in Germany, policy interaction can achieve zero inflation in Europe as a whole. On the other hand, it causes an increase in both unemployment and the structural deficit. Given a common demand shock in Europe, policy interaction can achieve zero inflation, zero unemployment, and a zero structural deficit in each of the member countries. Given a common supply shock in Europe, policy interaction can achieve zero inflation in each of the member countries. On the other hand, it causes an increase in both unemployment and the structural deficit.

2.2. Cooperation between European Central Bank, German Government, and French Government

The targets of policy cooperation are zero inflation, zero unemployment, and a zero structural deficit in each of the member countries. The instruments of policy cooperation are European money supply, German government purchases, and French government purchases. We assume that the policy makers agree on a common loss function. The amount of loss depends on inflation, unemployment, and the structural deficit in each of the member countries. The policy makers set European money supply, German government purchases, and French government purchases so as to minimize the common loss.

The cooperative equilibrium is determined by the first-order conditions for a minimum loss. It yields the optimum levels of European money supply, German government purchases, and French government purchases. Given a demand shock in Germany, policy cooperation can achieve zero inflation, zero unemployment, and a zero structural deficit in Europe as a whole. However, it cannot do so in Germany and France. Given a supply shock in Germany, policy cooperation is ineffective. Given a common demand shock in Europe, policy cooperation can achieve zero inflation, zero unemployment, and a zero structural deficit in each of the member countries. Given a common supply shock in Europe, policy cooperation is ineffective.

Symbols

A	autonomous term for Europe
A_1	autonomous term for Germany
A_2	autonomous term for France
B	autonomous term for Europe
B_1	autonomous term for Germany
B_2	autonomous term for France
G	European government purchases
G_1	German government purchases
G_2	French government purchases
L	loss, loss function
M	European money supply
T	European tax revenue at full-employment output
T_1	German tax revenue at full-employment output
T_2	French tax revenue at full-employment output
$\overline{Y}$	full-employment output in Europe
s	structural deficit ratio in Europe
s_1	structural deficit ratio in Germany
s_2	structural deficit ratio in France
u	rate of unemployment in Europe
u_1	rate of unemployment in Germany
u_2	rate of unemployment in France
α	monetary policy multiplier (unemployment)
$\alpha\varepsilon$	monetary policy multiplier (inflation)
β	fiscal policy multiplier (unemployment)
$\beta\varepsilon$	fiscal policy multiplier (inflation)
γ	monetary policy multiplier (inflation)
δ	fiscal policy multiplier (inflation)
π	rate of inflation in Europe
π_1	rate of inflation in Germany
π_2	rate of inflation in France

The Current Research Project

The present book is part of a larger research project on monetary union, see Carlberg (1999, 2000, 2001, 2002, 2003, 2004, 2005, 2006a, 2006b, 2007, 2008). Volume two (2000) deals with the scope and limits of macroeconomic policy in a monetary union. The leading protagonists are the union central bank, national governments, and national trade unions. Special emphasis is put on wage shocks and wage restraint. This book develops a series of basic, intermediate and more advanced models. A striking feature is the numerical estimation of policy multipliers. A lot of diagrams serve to illustrate the subject in hand. The monetary union is an open economy with high capital mobility. The exchange rate between the monetary union and the rest of the world is flexible. The world interest rate can be exogenous or endogenous. The union countries may differ in money demand, consumption, imports, openness, or size.

Volume three (2001) explores the new economics of monetary union. It discusses the effects of shocks and policies on output and prices. Shocks and policies are country-specific or common. They occur on the demand or supply side. Countries can differ in behavioural functions. Wages can be fixed, flexible, or slow. In addition, fixed wages and flexible wages can coexist. Take for instance fixed wages in Germany and flexible wages in France. Or take fixed wages in Europe and flexible wages in America. Throughout this book makes use of the rate-of-growth method. This method, together with suitable initial conditions, proves to be very powerful. Further topics are inflation and disinflation. Take for instance inflation in Germany and price stability in France. Then what policy is needed for disinflation in the union? And what will be the dynamic effects on Germany and France?

Volume four (2002) deals with the causes and cures of inflation in a monetary union. It studies the effects of money growth and output growth on inflation. The focus is on producer inflation, currency depreciation and consumer inflation. For instance, what determines the rate of consumer inflation in Europe, and what in America? Moreover, what determines the rate of consumer inflation in Germany, and what in France? Further issues are real depreciation, nominal and real interest rates, the growth of nominal wages, the growth of producer real wages, and the growth of consumer real wages. Here productivity growth and labour growth play significant roles. Another issue is target inflation and required money growth. A prominent feature of this book is microfoundations for a monetary union.

Volume five (2003) deals with the international coordination of economic policy in a monetary union. It discusses the process of policy competition and the structure of policy cooperation. As to policy competition, the focus is on competition between the union central bank, the German government, and the French government. Similarly, as to policy cooperation, the focus is on cooperation between the union central bank, the German government, and the French government. The key questions are: Does the process of policy competition lead to price stability and full employment? Can these targets be achieved through policy cooperation? And is policy cooperation superior to policy competition?

Volume six (2004) studies the interactions between monetary and fiscal policies in the euro area. The policy makers are the union central bank, the German government, the French government, and other governments. The policy targets are price stability in the union, full employment in Germany, full employment in France, etc. The policy instruments are union money supply, German government purchases, French government purchases, etc. As a rule, the spillovers of fiscal policy are negative. The policy makers follow either cold-turkey or gradualist strategies. The policy decisions are taken sequentially or simultaneously. Policy expectations are adaptive or rational. This book carefully discusses the case for central bank independence and fiscal cooperation.

Volume seven (2005) deals with the international coordination of monetary and fiscal policies in the world economy. It examines the process of policy competition and the structure of policy cooperation. As to policy competition, the focus is on monetary and fiscal competition between Europe and America. Similarly, as to policy cooperation, the focus is on monetary and fiscal cooperation between Europe and America. The spillover effects of monetary policy are negative while the spillover effects of fiscal policy are positive. The policy targets are price stability and full employment. The policy makers follow either cold-turkey or gradualist strategies. Policy expectations are adaptive or rational. The world economy consists of two, three or more regions.

Volume eight (2006a) further studies the interactions between monetary and fiscal policies in the euro area. It discusses the process of policy competition and the structure of policy cooperation. As to policy competition, the focus is on competition between the European central bank, the American central bank, the German government, and the French government. As to policy cooperation, the focus is on the same institutions. These are higher-dimensional issues. The policy targets are price stability and full employment. The policy makers follow cold-turkey or gradualist strategies. The policy decisions are taken sequentially or simultaneously. Monetary and fiscal policies have spillover effects. Special features of this book are numerical simulations of policy competition and numerical solutions to policy cooperation.

Volume nine (2006b) deals with the interactions between monetary and wage policies in the euro area. It examines the process of policy competition and the structure of policy cooperation. As to policy competition, the focus is on competition between the European central bank, the American central bank, the German labour union, and the French labour union. As to policy cooperation, the focus is on the same institutions. These are higher-dimensional issues. The policy targets are price stability and full employment. The policy makers follow cold-turkey or gradualist strategies. The policy decisions are taken sequentially or simultaneously. Monetary and wage policies have spillover effects. Special features of this book are numerical simulations of policy competition and numerical solutions to policy cooperation.

Volume ten (2007), unlike other books, provides readers with a practical yet sophisticated grasp of the macroeconomic principles necessary to understand a monetary union. By definition, a monetary union is a group of countries that share a common currency. The most important case in point is the euro area. Policy makers are the central bank, national governments, and national labour unions. Policy targets are price stability and full employment. Policy makers follow cold-turkey or gradualist strategies. Policy decisions are taken sequentially or simultaneously. The countries can differ in size or behaviour. Policy expectations are adaptive or rational. To illustrate all of this there are numerical simulations of monetary policy, fiscal policy, and wage policy.

Volume eleven studies the coexistence of inflation and unemployment in a monetary union. The focus is on how to reduce the associated loss. The primary target of the European central bank is low inflation in Europe. The primary target of the German government is low unemployment in Germany. And the primary target of the French government is low unemployment in France. The European central bank has a quadratic loss function. The same applies to the German government and the French government. The key questions are: To what extent can the sequential process of monetary and fiscal decisions reduce the loss caused by inflation and unemployment? Is monetary and fiscal cooperation superior to the sequential process of monetary and fiscal decisions?

Further information about these books is given on the web-page: http://carlberg.hsu-hh.de

References

ALESINA, A., BLANCHARD, O., GALI, J., GIAVAZZI, F., UHLIG, H., Defining a Macroeconomic Framework for the Euro Area, London 2001

ALESINA, A., GIAVAZZI, F., The Future of Europe: Reform or Decline, Cambridge 2006

ALLSOPP, C., The Coordination of Monetary, Fiscal and Labour Market Policies in the Euro Area, in: I. Begg, ed., Europe: Government and Money, London 2002

ALLSOPP, C., ARTIS, M., eds., EMU, Four Years On, in: Oxford Review of Economic Policy 19:1, 2003

ANDERSEN, T. M., Fiscal Stabilization Policy in a Monetary Union with Inflation Targeting, University of Aarhus 2002

ANGELONI, I., KASHYAP, A., MOJON, B., eds., Monetary Policy Transmission in the Euro Area, Cambridge 2003

ARESTIS, P., SAWYER, M., Reexamining Monetary and Fiscal Policy for the 21st Century, Cheltenham 2004

ARTIS, M., NIXSON, F., eds., The Economics of the European Union, Oxford 2001

ASADA, T., CHIARELLA, C., FLASCHEL, P., FRANKE, R., Open Economy Macrodynamics, Berlin 2003

BAIMBRIDGE, M., WHYMAN, P., eds., Economic and Monetary Union in Europe, Cheltenham 2003

BALDWIN, R., BERTOLA, G., SEABRIGHT, P., eds., EMU: Assessing the Impact of the Euro, Oxford 2003

BALL, L., Policy Rules for Open Economies, in: J. B. Taylor, ed., Monetary Policy Rules, Chicago 1999

BARRELL, R., WEALE, M., Monetary and Fiscal Coordination in the Euro Area, in: I. Begg, ed., Europe: Government and Money, London 2002

BEAN, C., Economic and Monetary Union in Europe, in: Journal of Economic Perspectives 6, 1992, 31 - 52

BEAN, C., Monetary Policy under EMU, in: Oxford Review of Economic Policy 14(3), 1998, 41 - 53

BEETSMA, R., et al., eds., Monetary Policy, Fiscal Policies and Labour Markets, Cambridge 2004

BEETSMA, R., DEBRUN, X., The Interaction between Monetary and Fiscal Policies in a Monetary Union: A Review of Recent Literature, in: R. Beetsma et al., eds., Monetary Policy, Cambridge 2004

BEETSMA, R., DEBRUN, X., KLAASSEN, F., Is Fiscal Policy Coordination in EMU Desirable?, in: Swedish Economic Policy Review 8, 2001, 57 - 98

BEGG, D., CANOVA, F., DE GRAUWE, P., FATAS, A., LANE, P., Surviving the Slowdown, London 2002

BEGG, I., ed., Europe: Government and Money: Running EMU: The Challenges of Policy Coordination, London 2002

BELKE, A., DUWENDAG, D., GROS, D., KÖSTERS, W., POHL, R., Geldtheorie und Geldpolitik in Europa, Berlin 2007

BERNANKE, B. S., WOODFORD, M., eds., The Inflation-Targeting Debate, Chicago 2005

BERTOLA, G., BOERI, T., EMU Labour Markets Two Years On, in: M. Buti, A. Sapir, eds., EMU and Economic Policy in Europe, Cheltenham 2002

BINI SMAGHI, L., GROS, D., Open Issues in European Central Banking, London 2000

BLANCHARD, O., Macroeconomics, Upper Saddle River 2003

BLINDER, A. S., Central Banking in Theory and Practice, Cambridge 1998

BOFINGER, P., Monetary Policy, Oxford 2001

BOYER, R., Coordination of Economic Policies in Europe, in: I. Begg, ed., Europe: Government and Money, London 2002

BRANSON, H. W., HENDERSON, D. W., GOLDSTEIN, M., eds., International Policy Coordination and Exchange Rate Fluctuations, Chicago 1990

BREUSS, F., Monetäre Außenwirtschaft und Europäische Integration, Frankfurt 2006

BREUSS, F., FINK, G., GRILLER, S., eds., Institutional, Legal and Economic Aspects of the EMU, Berlin 2003

BRUNILA, A., BUTI, M., FRANCO, D., eds., The Stability and Growth Pact, Houndmills 2001

BRYANT, R., The Coordination of National Stabilization Policies, in: A. Hughes Hallett et al., eds., Challenges for Economic Policy Coordination within European Monetary Union, Dordrecht 2001

BRYANT, R., International Coordination of National Stabilization Policies, Washington 1995

BRYSON, J. H., Macroeconomic Stabilization Through Monetary and Fiscal Policy Coordination: Implications for European Monetary Union, in: Open Economies Review 5, 1994, 307 - 326

BRYSON, J., JENSEN, H., VAN HOOSE, D., Rules, Discretion and International Monetary and Fiscal Policy Coordination, in: Open Economies Review 4, 1993, 117-132

BUITER, W. H., The Economic Case for Monetary Union in the European Union, in: Review of International Economics 5(4), 1997, 10 - 35

BUITER, W. H., GRAFE, C., Reforming EMU's Fiscal Policy Rules, in: M. Buti, ed., Monetary and Fiscal Policies in EMU, Cambridge 2003

BUITER, W. H., MARSTON, R. C., eds., International Economic Policy Coordination, Cambridge 1985

BURDA, M., European Labour Markets and the Euro: How Much Flexibility Do We Really Need?, in: Deutsche Bundesbank, ed., The Monetary Transmission Process, Hondmills 2001

BURDA, M., WYPLOSZ, C., Macroeconomics, Oxford 2005

BUTI, M., ed., Monetary and Fiscal Policies in EMU: Interactions and Coordination, Cambridge 2003

BUTI, M., FRANCO, D., Fiscal Policy in EMU, Cheltenham 2005

BUTI, M., ROEGER, W., INTVELD, J., Stabilising Output and Inflation in EMU: Policy Conflicts and Cooperation under the Stability Pact, European Commission 2001

BUTI, M., SAPIR, A., eds., Economic Policy in EMU, Oxford 1998

BUTI, M., SAPIR, A., eds., EMU and Economic Policy in Europe: The Challenge of the Early Years, Cheltenham 2002

BUTI, M., VON HAGEN, J., MARTINEZ-MONGAY, C., eds., The Behaviour of Fiscal Authorities, Houndmills 2002

CALMFORS, L., et al., EMU - A Swedish Perspective, Dordrecht 1997

CANOVA, F., PAPPA, E., Does it Cost to be Virtous? The Macroeconomic Effects of Fiscal Constraints, in: NBER International Seminar on Macroeconomics 2004, Cambridge, Mass. 2006

CANZONERI, M. B., CUMBY, R. E., DIBA, B. T., How Do Monetary and Fiscal Policy Interact in the European Monetary Union, in: NBER International Seminar on Macroeconomics 2004, Cambridge, Mass. 2006

CANZONERI, M. B., CUMBY, R. E., DIBA, B., New Views on the Transatlantic Transmission of Fiscal Policy and Macroeconomic Policy

Coordination, in: M. Buti, ed., Monetary and Fiscal Policies in EMU, Cambridge 2003

CANZONERI, M. B., DIBA, B. T., The Stability and Growth Pact: A Delicate Balance or an Albatross?, in: A. Hughes Hallett et al., eds., Challenges for Economic Policy Coordination within European Monetary Union, Dordrecht 2001

CANZONERI, M. B., HENDERSON, D. W., Monetary Policy in Interdependent Economies, Cambridge 1991

CARLBERG, M., An Economic Analysis of Monetary Union, Berlin New York 2001

CARLBERG, M., Economic Policy in a Monetary Union, Berlin New York 2000

CARLBERG, M., Inflation and Unemployment in a Monetary Union, Berlin 2008

CARLBERG, M., Inflation in a Monetary Union, Berlin New York 2002

CARLBERG, M., International Economic Policy Coordination, Berlin New York 2005

CARLBERG, M., Macroeconomics of Monetary Union, Berlin New York 2007

CARLBERG, M., Monetary and Fiscal Policies in the Euro Area, Berlin New York 2006

CARLBERG, M., Monetary and Wage Policies in the Euro Area, Berlin New York 2006

CARLBERG, M., Policy Competition and Policy Cooperation in a Monetary Union, Berlin New York 2004

CARLBERG, M., Policy Coordination in a Monetary Union, Berlin New York 2003

CARRARO, C., et al., eds., International Economic Policy Coordination, Oxford 1991

CAVALLARI, L., Inflationary Performance in a Monetary Union with Large Wage Setters, in: R. Beetsma et al., eds., Monetary Policy, Cambridge 2004

CAVALLARI, L., DI GIOACHINO, D., Macroeconomic Stabilization in the EMU: Rules versus Institutions, in: Review of Development Economics 9, 264-276, 2005

CHARI, V.V., KEHOE, P., On the Need for Fiscal Constraints in a Monetary Union, Working Paper no. 589, Federal Reserve Bank of Minneapolis 1998

CHOI, J. J., WRASE, J. M., eds., European Monetary Union and Capital Markets, Amsterdam 2001

CLAUSEN, V., Asymmetric Monetary Transmission in Europe, Berlin 2001

COLLIGNON, S., Monetary Stability in Europe, London 2002

COOPER, R. N., Economic Interdependence and Coordination of Economic Policies, in: R. W. Jones, P. B. Kenen, eds., Handbook of International Economics, Amsterdam 1985

COOPER, R., KEMPF, H., Designing Stabilization Policy in a Monetary Union, NBER Working Paper No. 7607, 2000

CUKIERMAN, A., Monetary Institutions, Monetary Union, and Unionised Labour Markets, in: R. Beetsma et al., eds., Monetary Policy, Cambridge 2004

DASEKING, C., Makroökonomische Interdependenzen in einer Wechselkursunion, Frankfurt 1994

DE BONIS, V., Stabilization Policy in an Exchange Rate Union, Heidelberg 1994

DEBRUN, X., Macroeconomic Policies in the European Monetary Union: Credibility, Coordination and Institutions, PhD Dissertation, University of Geneva 1999

DE GRAUWE, P., Economics of Monetary Union, Oxford 2005

DE HAAN, J., EIJFFINGER, S., WALLER, S., The European Central Bank: Credibility, Transparency, and Centralization, Cambridge 2005

DEMERTZIS, M., HUGHES HALLETT, A., VIEGI, N., Can the ECB be Truly Independent? Should It Be?, in: A. Hughes Hallett et al., eds., Challenges for Economic Policy Coordination within European Monetary Union, Dordrecht 2001

DEROOSE, S., LANGEDIJK, S., Economic Policy Coordination in EMU: Accomplishments and Challenges, in: M. Buti, A. Sapir, eds., EMU and Economic Policy in Europe, Cheltenham 2002

DEUTSCHE BUNDESBANK, ed., The Monetary Transmission Process: Recent Developments and Lessons for Europe, Houndmills 2001

DIXIT, A., Games of Monetary and Fiscal Interactions in the EMU, in: European Economic Review 45, 2001, 589-613

DIXIT, A., LAMBERTINI, L., Monetary-Fiscal Policy Interactions and Commitment versus Discretion in a Monetary Union, in: European Economic Review 45, 2001, 977-987

DORNBUSCH, R., FISCHER, S., STARTZ, R., Macroeconomics, New York 2001

DULLIEN, S., The Interaction of Monetary Policy and Wage Bargaining in the European Monetary Union, Houndmills 2004

DUWENDAG, D., KETTERER, K. H., KÖSTERS, W., POHL, R., SIMMERT, D. B., Geldtheorie und Geldpolitik in Europa, Berlin 1999

EICHENGREEN, B., European Monetary Unification, Cambridge 1997

EIJFFINGER, S., DE HAAN, J., European Monetary and Fiscal Policy, Oxford 2000

EUROPEAN CENTRAL BANK, Fiscal Policy Influences on Macroeconomic Stability and Prices, in: Monthly Bulletin, April 2004

EUROPEAN CENTRAL BANK, The Monetary Policy of the ECB, Frankfurt 2004

EUROPEAN CENTRAL BANK, The Relationship between Monetary Policy and Fiscal Policies in the Euro Area, in: Monthly Bulletin, February 2003

FATAS, A., MIHOV, I., Fiscal Policy and EMU, in: M. Buti, A. Sapir, eds., EMU and Economic Policy in Europe, Cheltenham 2002

FAVERO, C., et al., One Money, Many Countries, London 2000

FELDSTEIN, M., The European Central Bank and the Euro: The First Year, in: Journal of Policy Modeling 22, 2000, 345 – 354

FELDSTEIN, M., ed., International Economic Cooperation, Chicago 1988

FEUERSTEIN, S., Studien zur Wechselkursunion, Heidelberg 1992

FEUERSTEIN, S., SIEBKE, J., Wechselkursunion und Stabilitätspolitik, in: Zeitschrift für Wirtschafts- und Sozialwissenschaften 110, 1990, 359 – 379

FISCHER, S., International Macroeconomic Policy Coordination, in: M. Feldstein, ed., International Economic Cooperation, Chicago 1988

FISCHER, S., Roundtable on Lessons of European Monetary Integration for the International Monetary System, in: P. R. Masson et al., eds., EMU, Washington 1997

FLEMING, J. M., Domestic Financial Policies under Fixed and Floating Exchange Rates, in: IMF Staff Papers 9, 1962, 369 - 380

FRATIANNI, M., SALVATORE, D., VON HAGEN, J., eds., Macroeconomic Policy in Open Economies, Westport 1997

FRIEDMAN, B. M., HAHN, F. H., eds., Handbook of Monetary Economics, Amsterdam 1990

GALI, J., Monetary Policy in the Early Years of EMU, in: M. Buti, A Sapir, eds., EMU and Economic Policy in Europe, Cheltenham 2002

GALI, J., GERTLER, M., LOPEZ-SALIDO, J. D., European Inflation Dynamics, in: European Economic Review 45, 2001, 1237 – 1270

GANDOLFO, G., International Finance and Open-Economy Macroeconomics, Berlin 2001

GASPAR, V., ISSING, O., TRISTANI, O., VESTIN, D., Imperfect Knowledge and Monetary Policy, Cambridge 2006

GHOSH, A., MASSON, P., Economic Cooperation in an Uncertain World, Cambridge 1994

GIOVANNINI, A., et al., The Monetary Future of Europe, London 1993

GROS, D., ed., Macroeconomic Policy under the Euro, Cheltenham 2004

HALL, S. G., HEILEMANN, U., PAULY, P., eds., Macroeconometric Models and European Monetary Union, Berlin 2004

HAMADA, K., The Political Economy of International Monetary Interdependence, Cambridge 1985

HAMADA, K., KAWAI, M., International Economic Policy Coordination: Theory and Policy Implications, in: M. U. Fratianni, D. Salvatore, J. von Hagen, eds. Macroeconomic Policy in Open Economies, Westport 1997

HANSEN, J. D., HEINRICH, H., NIELSEN, J. U., An Economic Analysis of the EC, London 1992

HANSEN, J. D., NIELSEN, J. U., An Economic Analysis of the EU, London 1997

HEFEKER, C., Lohnpolitik und Geldpolitik in Euroland, in: Vierteljahreshefte zur Wirtschaftsforschung, 71. Jahrgang, Heft 3, 2002

HEIJDRA, B. J., VAN DER PLOEG, F., Foundations of Modern Macroeconomics, Oxford 2002

HEISE, A., Theorie optimaler Lohnräume – Zur Tarifpolitik in der Europäischen Währungsunion, in: Vierteljahreshefte zur Wirtschaftsforschung, 71. Jahrgang, Heft 3, 2002

HUART, F., Spillover Effects of Fiscal Policy in EMU: A Misconception behind the Stability Pact, Discussion Paper, Lille 2002

HUGHES HALLET, A., HUTCHISON, M. M., JENSEN, S. H., eds., Fiscal Aspects of European Monetary Integration, Cambridge 1999

HUGHES HALLET, A., McADAM, P., The Stability Pact and the Interdependence of Monetary and Fiscal Policy Rules, in: A. Hughes Hallet et al., eds., Challenges for Economic Policy Coordination within European Monetary Union, Dordrecht 2001

HUGHES HALLET, A., MOOSLECHNER, P., SCHUERZ, M., eds., Challenges for Economic Policy Coordination within European Monetary Union, Dordrecht 2001

ILLING, G., Theorie der Geldpolitik, Berlin 1997

ISSING, O., On Macroeconomic Policy Coordination in EMU, in: Journal of Common Market Studies 40, 2002

ISSING, O., GASPAR, V., ANGELONI, I., TRISTANI, O., Monetary Policy in the Euro Area, Cambridge 2001

ITALIANER, A., The Euro and Internal Economic Policy Coordination, in: A. Hughes Hallett et al., eds., Challenges for Economic Policy Coordination within European Monetary Union, Dordrecht 2001

JACQUET, P., PISANI-FERRY, J., Economic Policy Coordination in the Euro Zone, Paris 2000

JARCHOW, H. J., Fiskalpolitik in einer Währungsunion, in: Finanzarchiv 50, 1993, 187 - 203

JARCHOW, H. J., RÜHMANN, P., Monetäre Außenwirtschaft, Göttingen 2003

KEHOE, P. J., Coordination of Fiscal Policies in a World Economy, in: Journal of Monetary Economics 19, 1987, 349-376

KENEN, P. B., Economic and Monetary Union in Europe, Cambridge 1995

KOPCKE, R. W., TOOTELL, G. M. B., TRIEST, R. K., eds., The Macroeconomics of Fiscal Policy, Cambridge 2006

KRUGMAN, P. R., OBSTFELD, M., International Economics, New York 2003

LAMBERTINI, L., ROVELLI, R., Independent or Coordinated? Monetary and Fiscal Policy in EMU, in: R. Beetsma et al., eds., Monetary Policy, Cambridge 2004

LANE, P.R., Monetary-Fiscal Interactions in an Uncertain World, in: M. Buti, ed., Monetary and Fiscal Policy in EMU, Cambridge 2003

LAWLER, P., Monetary Policy and Asymmetrical Fiscal Policy in a Jointly Floating Currency Area, in: Scottish Journal of Political Economy 41, 1994, 142 - 162

LEIDERMAN, L., SVENSSON, L., eds., Inflation Targeting, London 1995

LEVIN, J. H., On the Dynamic Effects of Monetary and Fiscal Policy in a Monetary Union, in: K. V. Maskus et al., eds., Quiet Pioneering, Michigan 1997

LEVIN, J. H., A Guide to the Euro, Boston 2002

LEVIN, J. H., A Model of Stabilization Policy in a Jointly Floating Currency Area, in: J. S. Bhandari, B. H. Putnam, eds., Economic Interdependence and Flexible Exchange Rates, Cambridge 1983

LEVINE, P., Fiscal Policy Coordination under EMU and the Choice of Monetary Instrument, in: Manchester School 61, Supplement, 1993, 1-12

LEVINE, P., BROCINER, A., Fiscal Policy Coordination and EMU, in: Journal of Economic Dynamics and Control 18, 1994, 699-729

MARK, N. C., International Macroeconomics and Finance, Oxford 2001

MASSON, P. R., KRUEGER, T.H., TURTELBOOM, B. G., eds., EMU and the International Monetary System, Washington 1997

McCALLUM, B. T., International Monetary Economics, Oxford 1995

McKIBBIN, W. J., Empirical Evidence on International Economic Policy Coordination, in: M. U. Fratianni, D. Salvatore, J. von Hagen, eds., Macroeconomic Policy in Open Economies, Westport 1997

MEADE, J., WEALE, M., Monetary Union and the Assignment Problem, in: Scandinavian Journal of Economics 97, 1995, 201-222

MICHAELIS, J., PFLÜGER, M., Euroland: Besser als befürchtet, aber schlechter als erhofft?, in: Vierteljahreshefte zur Wirtschaftsforschung, 71. Jahrgang, Heft 3, 2002

MOOSLECHNER, P., SCHUERZ, M., International Macroeconomic Policy Coordination: Any Lessons for EMU? A Selective Survey of the Literature, in: A. Hughes Hallett et al., eds., Challenges for Economic Policy Coordination within European Monetary Union, Dordrecht 2001

MOSER, T., SCHIPS, B., eds., EMU, Financial Markets and the World Economy, Dordrecht 2001

MOUTOS, T., SCARTH, W., Stabilization Policy within a Currency Area, in: Scottish Journal of Political Economy 35, 1988, 387 – 397

MULHEARN, C., VANE, H. R., The Euro, Cheltenham 2008

MUNDELL, R. A., International Economics, New York 1968

MUNDELL, R. A., CLESSE, A., eds., The Euro as a Stabilizer in the International Economic System, Dordrecht 2000

MUNDELL, R.A., ZAK, P. J., SCHAEFFER, D., eds., International Monetary Policy after the Euro, Cheltenham 2005

NECK, R., ed., The Macroeconomics of EMU, in: Open Economies Review 13:4, 2002

NECK, R., HABER, G., McKIBBIN, J., European Monetary and Fiscal Policies after the EU Enlargement, in: Empirica 31, 2004, 229 – 245

NECK, R., HOLZMANN, R., eds., European Monetary and Fiscal Policies: Myths and Facts, in: Empirica 29:3, 2002

NECK, R., RICHTER, C., MOOSLECHNER, P., Quantitative Economic Policy, Berlin 2008

NEUMANN, M. J. M., Internationale Wirtschaftspolitik: Koordination, Kooperation oder Wettbewerb?, in: J. Siebke, Hg., Monetäre Konfliktfelder der Weltwirtschaft, Berlin 1991

NEUMANN, M. J. M., Koordination der Makropolitik in Europa, in: B. Gahlen, H. Hesse, H. J. Ramser, Hg., Europäische Integrationsprobleme, Tübingen 1994

OBSTFELD, M., ROGOFF, K., Foundations of International Macroeconomics, Cambridge 1996

OECD, EMU: Facts, Challenges and Policies, Paris 1999

OECD, EMU: One Year On, Paris 2000

OHR, R., THEURL, T., Hg., Kompendium Europäische Wirtschaftspolitik, München 2000

ONORANTE, L., Interaction of Fiscal Policies in the Euro Area: How Much Pressure on the ECB?, in: R. Beetsma et al., eds., Monetary Policy, Cambridge 2004

PADOAN, P. C., Monetary Policy is not Enough: Pressures for Policy Change in EMU, in: I. Begg, ed., Europe: Government and Money, London 2002

PADOAN, P. C., ed., Monetary Union, Employment and Growth, Cheltenham 2001

PADOA-SCHIOPPA, T., The Euro and Its Central Bank, Cambridge 2004

PENTECOST, E. J., VAN POECK, A., eds., European Monetary Integration, Cheltenham 2001

PERSSON, T., TABELLINI, G., Political Economics, Cambridge 2000

PICHELMANN, K., Wage Discipline in EMU, in: M. Buti, A. Sapir, eds., EMU and Economic Policy in Europe, Cheltenham 2002

PISANI-FERRY, J., The EMU's Economic Policy Principles: Words and Facts, in: M. Buti, A. Sapir, eds., EMU and Economic Policy in Europe, Cheltenham 2002

PLASMANS, J., et al., Dynamic Modeling of Monetary and Fiscal Cooperation among Nations, Berlin 2005

POHL, R., GALLER, H. P., eds., Macroeconometric Modelling of the German Economy in the Framework of Euroland, Baden-Baden 2002

POSEN, A. S., ed., The Euro at Five: Ready for a Global Role? Washington 2005

ROSE, K., SAUERNHEIMER, K., Theorie der Außenwirtschaft, München 2006

ROSE, K., SAUERNHEIMER, K., Zur Theorie eines Mischwechselkurssystems, in: M. Feldsieper, R. Groß, Hg., Wirtschaftspolitik in weltoffener Wirtschaft, Berlin 1983, 15 - 28

RÜBEL, G., Grundlagen der Monetären Außenwirtschaft, München 2005

SALVATORE, D., The Euro, the Dollar, and the International Monetary System, in: Journal of Policy Modeling 22, 2000, 407 – 415

SAPIR, A., et al., An Agenda for a Growing Europe, Oxford 2004

SARNO, L., TAYLOR, M., The Economics of Exchange Rates, Cambridge 2002

SAUERNHEIMER, K., Fiscal Policy in einer Wechselkursunion, in: Finanzarchiv 42, 1984, 143 - 157

SCHEIDE, J., Macroeconomic Policy Coordination in Europe, in: H. Siebert, ed., Macroeconomic Policies in the World Economy, Berlin 2004

SCHELKLE, W., Monetäre Integration, Heidelberg 2001

SEMMLER, W., GREINER, A., ZHANG, W., Monetary and Fiscal Policies in the Euro Area, Amsterdam 2005

SIDIROPOULOS, M., SPYROMITROS, E., Fiscal Policy in a Monetary Union under Alternative Labor Market Regimes, Discussion Paper, Strasbourg 2005

SIEBERT, H., Macroeconomic Policies in the World Economy, Berlin 2004

SINN, H. W., WIDGREN, M., KÖTHENBÜRGER, M., eds., European Monetary Integration, Cambridge 2004

SITZ, A., Währungsunion oder Wechselkursflexibilität, Frankfurt 2001

SMETS, J., DOMBRECHT, M., eds., How to Promote Economic Growth in the Euro Area, Cheltenham 2001

SPAHN, H. P., From Gold to Euro, Berlin 2001

SPAHN, H. P., Geldpolitik, München 2006

STABILISIERUNGSPOLITIK IN EUROLAND, in: Vierteljahreshefte zur Wirtschaftsforschung, 71. Jahrgang, Heft 3, 2002

STAHN, K., Reputation und Kooperation in einer Währungsunion, Frankfurt 2000

SUARDI, M., Monetary Policy Transmission in EMU, in: M. Buti, A. Sapir, eds., EMU and Economic Policy in Europe, Cheltenham 2002

SVENSSON, L. E. O., Monetary Policy Issues für the Eurosystem, in: Carnegie-Rochester Conference Series on Public Policy 51, 1999, 79 - 136

TAYLOR, J. B., ed., Monetary Policy Rules, Chicago 1999

TAYLOR, J. B., WOODFORD, M., eds., Handbook of Macroeconomics, Amsterdam 1999

TRUMAN, E. M., A Critical Review of Coordination Efforts in the Past, in: H. Siebert, ed., Macroeconomic Policies in the World Economy, Berlin 2004

UHLIG, H., One Money, but Many Fiscal Policies in Europe, in: M. Buti, ed., Monetary and Fiscal Policies in EMU, Cambridge 2003

VAN AARLE, B., GARRETSEN, H., HUART, F., Monetary and Fiscal Policy Rules in the EMU, Working Paper 2003

VAN AARLE, B., GARRETSEN, H., HUART, F., Transatlantic Monetary and Fiscal Policy Interaction, Working Paper 2003

VAN AARLE, B., WEYERSTRASS, K., eds., Economic Spillovers, Structural Reforms, and Policy Coordination in the Euro Area, Berlin 2008

VAN DER PLOEG, F., Macroeconomic Policy Coordination and Monetary Integration: A European Perspective, The Hague 1989

VIREN, M., Fiscal Policy, Automatic Stabilisers and Coordination, in: A. Brunila et al., eds., The Stability and Growth Pact, Houndmills 2001

VOLLMER, U., Geld- und Währungspolitik, München 2004

VON HAGEN, J., MUNDSCHENK, S., The Functioning of Economic Policy Coordination, in: M. Buti, A. Sapir, eds., EMU and Economic Policy in Europe, Cheltenham 2002

WALSH, C., Monetary Theory and Policy, Cambridge 2003

WELFENS, P. J. J., European Monetary Union and Exchange Rate Dynamics, Berlin 2000

WICKS, N., The Coordination of Economic Policies in the European Union, in I. Begg, ed., Europe: Government and Money, London 2002

WOHLTMANN, H. W., Transmission nationaler Wirtschaftspolitiken in einer Wechselkursunion, in: Jahrbücher für Nationalökonomie und Statistik 211, 1993, 73 – 89

WOHLTMANN, H. W., BULTHAUPT, F., KRÖMER, W., Wirtschaftspolitische Koordination in einer symmetrischen und asymmetrischen Wechselkursunion, in: K. Farmer, H. W. Wohltmann, Hg., Quantitative Wirtschaftspolitik, Münster 1998

WOODFORD, M., Interest and Prices, Princeton 2003

WYPLOSZ, C., ed., The Impact of EMU on Europe and the Developing Countries, Oxford 2001

Index

Budget deficit, see Structural deficit

Common demand shock in Europe, 104, 165
Common supply shock in Europe, 166
Comparing cases A and B, 112, 122, 153, 192
Comparing policy cooperation with policy interaction, 140, 202
Cooperation, 43, 90, 132, 193
Cooperation between central bank and government, 43, 90
Cooperation between European central bank, German government, and French government, 132, 193
Cooperative equilibrium, 45, 91, 134, 194
Cooperative equilibrium of European government purchases, 45, 91
Cooperative equilibrium of European inflation, 45, 91
Cooperative equilibrium of European money supply, 45, 91, 134, 194
Cooperative equilibrium of European structural deficit, 91
Cooperative equilibrium of European unemployment, 45, 91
Cooperative equilibrium of French government purchases, 134, 194
Cooperative equilibrium of French inflation, 135, 195
Cooperative equilibrium of French structural deficit, 196
Cooperative equilibrium of French unemployment, 135, 195
Cooperative equilibrium of German government purchases, 134, 194
Cooperative equilibrium of German inflation, 135, 195
Cooperative equilibrium of German structural deficit, 196
Cooperative equilibrium of German unemployment, 134, 195
Cooperative solution, multiple, see Multiple cooperative solutions
Cooperative solution, unique, see Unique cooperative solution

Deficit target, 57, 141
Degrees of freedom, 42, 44 - 45, 131, 134
Demand shock in Europe, 17, 22, 29, 46, 62, 74, 92, 104, 165
Demand shock in Germany, 101, 116, 136, 146, 161

European government purchases, 27, 32, 37, 43, 59, 65, 70, 77, 83, 90
European money supply, 15, 20, 37, 43, 70, 77, 83, 90, 97, 106, 124, 132, 154, 169, 181, 193

First-order conditions, 20, 32, 44, 65, 90, 99, 106, 134, 157, 182, 194
Fiscal policy, 27, 32, 59, 65, 114, 119, 143, 149
Fiscal policy in Germany, 114, 119, 143, 149
French government purchases, 124, 132, 154, 169, 181, 193

German government purchases, 114, 119, 124, 132, 143, 149, 154, 169, 181, 193
Government purchases
   see European government purchases
   see French government purchases
   see German government purchases
Government purchases, optimum, see Optimum government purchases

Inefficiency, Pareto, 165, 178
Inflation in Europe, 15, 20, 27, 32, 37, 43, 59, 65, 70, 77, 83, 90
Inflation, optimum, see Optimum inflation
Interaction, 37, 50, 70, 77, 83, 124, 154, 169, 181
Interaction between central bank and government, 37, 50, 70, 77, 83
Interaction between European central bank, German government, and French government, 124, 154, 169, 181

Loss function of European central bank, 20, 39, 77, 98, 106, 126, 127, 156, 169
Loss function of European government, 32, 41, 60, 65, 71, 84
Loss function of French government, 130, 158, 183
Loss function of German government, 119, 129, 144, 149, 157, 182
Loss function under policy cooperation, 44, 90, 133, 193

Minimum loss, 20, 32, 44, 65, 90, 99, 106, 134, 157, 182, 194
Mixed shock in Europe, 24, 48
Mixed shock in Germany, 138
Monetary and fiscal cooperation, 43, 90, 132, 193
Monetary and fiscal interaction, 37, 50, 70, 77, 83, 124, 154, 169, 181
Monetary policy, 15, 20, 97, 106
Monetary policy in Europe, 97, 106

Monetary union as a whole, 13, 57
Monetary union of two countries, 95, 141
Money supply, see European money supply
Money supply, optimum, see Optimum money supply
Multiple cooperative solutions, 44 - 45, 134, 204 - 205
Multiple Nash equilibria, 42, 131, 204 - 205

Nash equilibrium, 38 - 42, 72, 78, 84, 127 - 131, 158, 171,183
Nash equilibrium of European government purchases, 72, 79, 85
Nash equilibrium of European inflation, 73, 79, 85
Nash equilibrium of European money supply, 72, 79, 85, 158, 172, 184
Nash equilibrium of European structural deficit, 73, 79, 85
Nash equilibrium of European unemployment, 72, 79, 85
Nash equilibrium of French government purchases, 158, 172, 184
Nash equilibrium of French inflation, 159, 173, 185
Nash equilibrium of French structural deficit, 160, 173, 185
Nash equilibrium of French unemployment, 159, 172, 184
Nash equilibrium of German government purchases, 158, 172, 184
Nash equilibrium of German inflation, 159, 172, 184
Nash equilibrium of German structural deficit, 160, 173, 185
Nash equilibrium of German unemployment, 159, 172, 184
Nash equilibrium, multiple, see Multiple Nash equilibria
Nash equilibrium, no, see No Nash equilibrium
Nash equilibrium, unique, see Unique Nash equilibrium
No Nash equilibrium, 39 - 42, 127 - 131, 204 - 205

Optimum government purchases, 28, 33, 45, 61, 66, 115, 119
Optimum inflation, 16, 21, 28, 33, 45, 61, 66, 99, 107, 115, 120, 135, 145, 150, 195
Optimum money supply, 16, 21, 45, 99, 107
Optimum structural deficit, 61, 66, 91, 145, 150, 196
Optimum unemployment, 16, 21, 28, 33, 45, 61, 66, 99, 107, 115, 120, 135, 145, 150, 195

Pareto inefficiency, 165, 178
Policy cooperation, 43, 90, 132, 193
Policy interaction, 37, 50, 70, 77, 83, 124, 154, 169, 181

Reaction function of European central bank, 38 - 41, 71, 78, 84, 126 - 130, 157, 170, 182
Reaction function of European government, 38 - 41, 72, 78, 84
Reaction function of French government, 126 - 130, 158, 171, 183
Reaction function of German government, 126 - 130, 157, 171, 183

Structural deficit, 59, 65, 70, 77, 83, 90, 143, 149, 154, 169, 181, 193
Structural deficit, optimum, see Optimum structural deficit
Summary, 104, 112, 117, 122, 131, 140, 148, 153, 167, 180, 192, 202
Supply shock in Europe, 18, 23, 30, 47, 63, 74, 93, 166
Supply shock in Germany, 102, 117, 138, 147, 163
Synopsis, 204

Targets of European central bank, 16, 38, 71, 98, 125, 156
Targets of European government, 28, 38, 60, 71
Targets of French government, 125, 156
Targets of German government, 115, 125, 144, 156
Targets of policy cooperation, 44, 90, 133, 193

Unemployment in Europe, 15, 20, 27, 32, 37, 43, 59, 65, 70, 77, 83, 90
Unemployment, optimum, see Optimum unemployment
Unique cooperative solution, 91, 194, 204 - 205
Unique Nash equilibrium, 72, 78, 84, 158, 172, 184, 204 - 205